New Testament
Basis of
Peacemaking

New Testament Basis of Peacemaking

Third Edition, Revised and Expanded

Richard McSorley

Foreword by John K. Stoner

A Christian Peace Shelf Selection

HERALD PRESS
Scottdale, Pennsylvania
Kitchener, Ontario

Library of Congress Cataloging in Publication Data

McSorley, Richard T., 1914-
  New Testament basis of peacemaking.

  "A Christian peace shelf selection."
  Bibliography: p.
  Includes index.
    1. Peace—Biblical teaching.   2. War—Biblical
teaching.   3. Peace—Religious aspects—Christianity—
History of doctrines.   4. War—Religious aspects—
Christianity—History of doctrines.   5. Bible.
N.T.—Criticism, interpretation, etc.   I. Title.
BS2545.P5M38   1985   261.8'73   84-25121
ISBN 0-8361-3383-8 (pbk.)

NEW TESTAMENT BASIS OF PEACEMAKING
Copyright © 1979, 1985 by Richard McSorley
Published by Herald Press, Scottdale, Pa. 15683
    Released simultaneously in Canada by Herald Press,
    Kitchener, Ont. N2G 4M5. All rights reserved.
Library of Congress Catalog Card Number: 84-25121
International Standard Book Number: 0-8361-3383-8
Printed in the United States of America
Design by Alice B. Shetler

90 89 88 87 86 85 10 9 8 7 6 5 4 3 2 1

Contents

Imprimatur by Bishop Carroll T. Dozier 9
Preface to Third Edition 10
Foreword by John K. Stoner 11

CHAPTER ONE
Does the New Testament Approve of War? 15
Five Principles
  First Principle: Love 17
  Second Principle: God Is Our Father/Mother 23
  Third Principle: The Almost Infinite Value of the
    Human Person 25
  Fourth Principle: Means and Ends Relationship 26
  Fifth Principle: Imitation of Christ .30

CHAPTER TWO
New Testament Texts Used for War .33
  John 2:14-16. In the temple he found those who
    were selling 33
  Matthew 26:52. For all who take the sword will
    perish by the sword. 34
  Matthew 10:34. I have not come to bring peace,
    but a sword. 35
  Matthew 8:5-13. A centurion came forward to him. 36
  Luke 11:21-22. When a strong man, fully armed,
    guards his own palace, his goods are in peace. 38
  John 15:13. Greater love has no man than this, that a
    man lay down his life for his friends. 38

Luke 22:36-38. And let him who has no sword sell his
    mantle and buy one. 39
Mark 12:13-17. Render to Caesar the things that
    are Caesar's, and to God the things that are God's. 43
Romans 13:1-7. Let every person be subject to the
    governing authorities 45

CHAPTER THREE
But Doesn't the Old Testament Allow Killing? 53
    The New Testament Fulfills the Old 53
    Holy War 56
    Old Testament Wars Are No Defense of Today's Wars . . .63
    God Alone Is the Author of Life 64
    We Are Stewards of God's Creation 66

CHAPTER FOUR
The First Three Centuries 68
    Characteristic Statements of Early Christian Writers 69

CHAPTER FIVE
The Just-Unjust War Theory 81
    Conditions of the Just-Unjust War Theory 82
    Weaknesses of the Just-Unjust War Theory 85
    Benefit of Doubt 93
    The Just Adultery Theory 99

CHAPTER SIX
Answers to Objections to Pacifism 103
    Argument 1. The Lesser Evil 104
    Argument 2. People Are Sinful 108
    Argument 3. Personal, Not Group Morality 109
    Argument 4. Self-Defense 110
    Argument 5. Protecting Your Loved Ones 113
    Argument 6. What About the Russians? 116
    Argument 7. Pacifism Is Not Practical 119
    Argument 8. What Alternative Is There? 120
    Argument 9. Unilateral Disarmament 122
    Argument 10. Saint Thomas Aquinas 124
    Argument 11. Obedience to Authority 127
    Argument 12. Spiritual Values Need Defense 128
    Argument 13. Vatican Council II Allows for a War of
    Self-Defense 130

Argument 14. Conscientious Objectors Are Cowards . . . 132
Argument 15. Deterrence Works 133
Argument 16. We Are Not All Children of God 135

CHAPTER SEVEN
The U.S. Bishops and the Bomb 141
    The Context 142
    What the Pastoral Letter Says 144
    What the Pastoral Letter Fails to Say 147
    The Implications for Us 151

Notes 153
Bibliography 155
Index 159
The Author 161
The Christian Peace Shelf 163

Imprimatur

Although the gospel message (of nonviolence) was never relaxed in theory, it was frequently neglected in practice as the church yielded to the tide of nationalism. Clergy blessed the guns on both sides, as Christians fought one another. The church's voice of peace has been largely hushed."

These words from my pastoral letter of 1971, *Peace: Gift and Task*, show the need of books relating to the gospel of peacemaking. On this topic, Catholic writers have trailed so far behind Protestants that it is difficult to find a book on the subject by a Catholic. That is some indication of the value of this book.

In my letter I gave a bird's-eye view of the history of Christian attitudes toward peace—three centuries of pacifism followed by St. Augustine's Just War Theory. This theory prevailed through the crusades up until modern times and, finally, into the nuclear age. In this nuclear age, we must "repudiate war as an instrument of national policy." This book enlarges that bird's-eye view, as it fills out many details, and offers answers to the age-old objections rising over against the gospel of love and peace.

I recommend this book, and hope that it will help us link our faith to our peace vision, so that we may understand that in working for peace we are instruments of God's love, and that our church is a peace church.

—Bishop Carroll T. Dozier, D.D.
Bishop of Memphis in Tennessee

Preface to Third Edition

The first two editions of this book were published by the Center for Peace Studies at Georgetown University. Without any paid advertising both editions sold out. But the Center's outreach is quite limited, so I thought I might extend its influence further with a more experienced and developed publisher like Herald Press.

I gave thought to changing the title because there are many improvements and additions to this edition, most of them made with the helpful suggestions of the theology book editor for Herald Press. In the end the decision was made to maintain the original title for the sake of continuity. This edition develops and enlarges both the gospel command "Love your enemy" and the gospel teaching that we are all children of God. In doing that, I am sensitive to the differences of theological opinion regarding this mysterious and wonderful truth. The Just-Unjust War Theory is treated more fully; some new objections against Christian nonviolence are proposed and answered. Finally, a whole new chapter on the U.S. Catholic Bishops Peace Pastoral was added.

I would like to thank Monica Cassidy, J. Patrick Cassidy, Chris Brown, and John Dear, S.J., for valued editorial and technical assistance, and Richard A. Kauffman of Herald Press, for his patience and cooperation.

—Richard McSorley, S.J.
May 27, 1984

Foreword

Readers of the Christian Peace Shelf will find this revised and expanded edition of Richard McSorley's *New Testament Basis of Peacemaking* a welcome addition to the Shelf. McSorley writes with the spontaneity of an engaging conversationalist and the wisdom of a philosopher and theologian. He can do this because as a person he is all of these and more. His writing is the overflow of a life of walking with God, of university teaching, and prophetic Christian pacifist witness.

The book offers a number of features unique among the volumes now available on the biblical basis for pacifism. These include McSorley's Five Principles setting forth the comprehensive basis for peacemaking in the New Testament, the Just-Unjust War Theory (which exhibits more candor and honesty than traditional just war discussions usually achieve), the Just Adultery Theory, and answers to 16 objections to pacifism.

Protestant and Catholic readers alike will profit from the author's chapter on the U.S. Bishops and the Bomb. The publication of "The Challenge of Peace: God's Promise and Our Response" in 1983 by the United States Conference of Catholic Bishops made history both in Catholic Church renewal and prophetic confrontation between church and state in the United States. The reverberations will continue for some time to come. McSorley gives a convincing analysis of what this document says, what it does not say, and its implications for us.

This publication of a Catholic author by a Mennonite publishing house is itself a sign of the new things which the Spirit of God is doing in the church. Common roots in Scripture are affirmed here. In addition, a common tradition of three hundred years of church history (the pre-Constantinian era) is affirmed. Old stereotypes of who is bearing faithful witness to Jesus Christ are outmoded. We must now hear every voice without prejudice and test what is said by the Word of God and the Spirit of Christ. For this we thank God.

A new unity in the body of Christ is being forged around the world. It is rooted in the experience of salvation by grace. Full salvation, that is, which believes that God saves us not only from the effects of our own sins, but also from the effects of the sins of others; not only from ourselves, but also from our enemies. I hear Richard McSorley telling us that although we can no more save ourselves from our enemies than we can save ourselves from our sins, God offers through Jesus Christ to save us from both.

—John K. Stoner, Chairman
The Christian Peace Shelf

New Testament
Basis of
Peacemaking

CHAPTER ONE

Does the New Testament Approve of War?

Since the fourth century, Christians have killed each other in so many wars that you might think that the gospel taught war, or at least approved of it. Because of the practice of war by Christians we rarely hear a sermon on how the gospel relates to war. Few Christians ask themselves the question, "Does the gospel approve of war?" The answer is assumed to be "yes" without any serious look at the gospel. The answer to that question is presumed to be "yes" because the thunderous "yes" of Christians fighting wars drowns out both the question and the gospel message of peace.

But that is changing now. Nuclear technology is forcing the change. We now live in a world threatened by thermonuclear destruction. One single twenty-megaton nuclear weapon dropped on New York would kill about seven million people. Carried on a rocket missile, it would take only twenty-four minutes to reach New York from Moscow.

We have no defense against nuclear weapons, nor have the Soviets. If they attack us, they die. If we attack them, we die. President Ronald Reagan noted this in a September 1983 speech at the United Nations: "A nuclear war cannot be won and must not be fought." Premier Yuri

Andropov in his reply said, "Responsible statesmen have only one choice—to do anything and everything possible to prevent a nuclear catastrophe. Any other position is short-sighted; more, it is suicidal."

We have about twenty-six thousand nuclear warheads; the Soviets have about twenty thousand. We would need to use only from two to four hundred delivered on target to destroy all Soviet cities of one hundred thousand or more. They would need about the same number delivered on target to destroy all U.S. cities of one hundred thousand or more. Yet, both of us continue to make more weapons. We make four new nuclear weapons each day, and plan to add seventeen thousand new weapons to our arsenal in the next five years. The Soviets race to match us.

It is this threat of nuclear disaster that causes many to turn to the gospel to see if there is not something there that might save us from the danger of nuclear war.

One way to get a focus on what the gospel says about war and peace is to ask ourselves the question, "Does the New Testament approve of war—not just nuclear war, but any war?" To make sense of that question, I have to explain what I mean by "war" because the word is used in many different ways (for example, war against poverty, war on drugs, etc.). Here is a working definition of war: "War is intergroup lethal conflict." It is not just a shoot-out on the street between two people, but rather, war pits group against group. To distinguish war further, we must add these characteristics: in war there is much killing; war has a momentum of its own that leads both sides to savagery unplanned by either side; and war involves a mobilization of group against group, spiritually and psychologically.

Now, using that definition, ask the question again about the gospel. Does the New Testament approve of intergroup lethal conflict that has as its characteristics much killing, a momentum of its own that leads both sides to unplanned savagery, and a mobilization of group against group?

Once you ask the question that way, you have your answer: "No, the gospel does not approve of war." The more clearly the definition is stated, the more obvious is the answer.

Why is this so? Why does the gospel disapprove of war? There are five principles of the gospel, so basic to the gospel, that they may be called "primary principles." They are: (1) love, (2) God is our Father/Mother, (3) the almost infinite value of the human person, (4) the relationship of agreement between means and end, and (5) the imitation of Christ. These principles are so basic to the gospel that if you denied any one of them, you would not have the gospel. All of them oppose war.

First Principle: Love

Jesus summarized all of his teaching in the command "Love God and your neighbor!" What he meant by neighbor is not vague or unclear. He meant to include everybody, even outcasts. This is clear from the parable of the Good Samaritan. In the United States today, neighbors include minority groups, blacks, Hispanics and Asians, and the anonymous poor.

Most mainline Christians would accept that. If I say, "I love the blacks, I love the whites, I love the poor, the children, the aged, and the handicapped," people will say, "Good! God bless you!"

But if I go further and say, in light of Jesus' command,

"Love your enemies," that "I love the Soviet Premier. . . . I love communists, and I want you, good Christian people, to love communists," they do not say, "God bless you!" Just the opposite! They will say, "Who let him in? Get the FBI! Run him out of here! He doesn't represent my faith!" It is in response to this command, "Love your enemy," that most mainline Christians part company with Jesus.

They don't say, "Jesus, we are not walking with you anymore." They are not that blunt. What they say goes something like this: "See that door there? Behind it are evil people. They are communists—evil people. They are planning to kill you. They are atheists! I look at you and see you are good people. You are peace people! You are believers in God! You are good Christians! I am going to save you." So they justify killing evil communists to save the rest of us who are good Christian folk!

That is a simple, elemental way of putting the Just-Unjust War Theory, a theory that says, "I can kill some to save others."

When I say that to fellow priests, and ask their opinions, I get the reply, "Under certain circumstances, you can kill some to save others. That is so," they say, "provided certain conditions are fulfilled, namely, that you save more than you kill and you do not kill the innocent. Under these and other conditions, killing is allowed. You show love by risking yourself to save others."

I answer, "But the gospel doesn't say we can kill to save others. Are you saying that in the act of killing communists, I am showing love to them? The gospel says, 'Love your enemy!' "

"No, you show love to those you save. I don't say you

can love and kill the same person in the same act. That is where the two theories differ—the theory of gospel non-violence, and the Just War Theory."

But the command "Love your enemy!" cannot be put aside lightly. It is not marginal or peripheral to our faith. It is central. When Jesus tells us, "Love your enemy," he is telling us to love others the way God loves us, unconditionally. God loves us when we are sinners. God loves us no matter what we have done, no matter what we will do. God loves us as we are, without conditions. That is the way God wants us to love others—unconditionally.

In giving this command, Jesus is trying to make our dull intellects understand from faith what we already know from experience—that genuine love seeks no return. We instinctively recognize true love when we experience it. And we do experience it from God, from a parent, from a close friend. It may not be continuous, but we do experience it. We don't need anyone to tell us the difference between true love and false love that comes only with love's name but without love's spiritual and emotional force. If I say, "I will love you if you give me $50 a week," you know that is not love. If I say, "I will love you as long as you appeal to me," that is not love because I am placing conditions on my love.

We sometimes experience within ourselves a capacity to love and to be loved unconditionally. Ask anyone, anywhere, anytime, "Do you want to be loved?" and they will answer without hesitation—certainly they want to be loved with a love that is perfect.

What does this mean and how is it applied to war? It means that my attitude toward my neighbor should not be determined by the damage done to me, or that might be done to me. It means I must respond in terms of the good of the person or the group involved. It is not a principle of do-nothing-under-attack, but rather, it is a principle that urges an active effort to express divine love by seeking the good of the enemy.

Active love is the response Jesus wants us to have even toward our enemies. Our love is to be independent of the attitude of the other person. We are to love simply because God wants us to reveal ourselves as true sons and daughters of our heavenly parent by this love.

"For if you love those who love you, what reward have you? Do not even the tax collectors do the same? And if you salute only your brethren, what more are you doing than others? Do not even the Gentiles do the same? (Mt. 5:46-48). In Jesus' teaching, all thought of reciprocity is excluded. We are not asked to love the Soviets because they love us, but because God loves us. When Jesus preached the Sermon on the Mount, he asked his followers to lead a certain way of life independently of what others might do. His words, "Blessed are you when men revile you and persecute you and utter all kinds of evil against you falsely on my account" (Mt. 5:11), make it clear that there is no demand for reciprocity in Jesus' love.

Both the promise of persecution and the command to "Love your enemies" illustrate the universality of the love Christ commands. This rules out killing one person to protect others. I cannot exclude even one person from my love. Such a love would not be universal. The common argument used to defend war ("We kill these people to defend others") has no foundation in the gospel. It violates the command of universal love. To comply with the law of universality, you have to argue that in the act of killing, you are showing love to the person you are killing.

That seems impossible to me—impossible and contradictory.

Some who defend war as compatible with Christian love argue that it is possible to kill and to destroy without feeling any hatred for the enemy. One response to this is that the absence of hate is not what the gospel asks. The gospel calls for positive, active love. Is it more virtuous to kill without hate than to kill with hate? The blinding power of hate may make killing without hate less culpable before God than a cold-blooded murder. Nonetheless, it is culpable; it is not the gospel.

A second response is that any use of force by a Christian is subject to conditions imposed by the gospel. These conditions are:

(1) Force can never be a substitute for the obligation to love.

(2) Any use of force makes love more difficult.

(3) Any use of force that is compatible with the gospel must be preparatory to and directed toward love for the person to whom the force is used. An example would be spanking a child with a few light taps that do no physical damage, but instruct the child about the danger of playing in the street.

(4) If the use of force is such that it makes any appeal to love impossible, then a Christian can never resort to it—for instance, spanking a child to death.

War does not fulfill these conditions. War kills. Death puts the person wholly beyond the reach of human love. The gospel calls for personal love. Modern warfare with its long-range lethal technology is so impersonal that any kind of personal relationship with the enemy is next to impossible. War poisons personal relationships by lying, trickery, and distrust of the enemy, simply because he or she is an enemy. Even the training for war illustrates this: it is a training in the depersonalization of both self and the enemy.

Military training puts all in the same uniform; teaches all to march, to turn, to reverse, to count steps, to count numbers; to eat, sleep, and to go when, where, and how according to orders.

It is a training in taking orders, even though they are monstrous and stupid orders, until you get to a point where you see yourself as a cog in the military machine. At that point you obey orders without question, even orders to kill. All of your training aims at helping you to obey without thought, without question. You no longer think of yourself as responsible for what you do. You no longer think of the target you shoot at as a person. You think of a person as a target, an obstacle, an enemy, a demon. Training in depersonalization prepares you to kill.

War is contrary to the gospel because war includes much killing. Killing leaves no room for the all-embracing love command.

Some who argue that the New Testament approves of war confuse police action with war. The two are not the same. Police action may escalate to a point where it is similar to war, especially in time of war. Ordinarily, there are clear patterns of difference. While police act within a limited area—their own country—the military move into other countries. While police aim to arrest, the military aims to kill or destroy individuals, groups, and even whole areas. While police use small weapons, and mostly nonlethal weapons, the military uses lethal weapons of mass destructive capacity. While police operate according to the laws of their country, the military operates in the jungle of international affairs.

Even if you believe that police action in general, for the sake of public order, is compatible with the gospel, police action is different enough from war that there is no contradiction in accepting one, and rejecting the other. Where police action becomes lethal, it becomes more like war, and becomes subject to the same disapproval as war.

Second Principle: God Is
Our Father/Mother

The New Testament teaches us that there is only one God, and that all of us are children of that one God. This is the basic theology of peace. It is taught by all the great religions of the world. It is so simple that a child can understand it.

The universalism expressed here seems at first glance to oppose the view that some personal response such as faith and obedience is required before one can be a child of God. But that opposition is not as great as it may seem at first. Even those who hold that faith and obedience are required to be a child of God would admit that we are all created by God, called by our creation to serve God and be with him forever.

There are various levels of meaning with the term "children of God." We are all redeemed in the blood of Christ. All of us are loved by God, and all of us are commanded to love each other, including enemies. We are commanded not to kill each other. Furthermore, none of these beliefs are dependent on whether or not we or others are obedient believers. In this way, it is clear that there are many meanings of the term "children of God." We are children of God by creation, by universal redemption, by common destiny to be with God, by baptism, and by response in faith and good works to God's call. Here I use the term in its broadest sense—our relation to God from creation. We are God's sons and daughters by creation and by the Creator's love for each of us.[1]

If we are all children of the one God, it follows that whenever I kill a human being anywhere, I kill a brother or sister. And whenever I kill a human being anywhere, I offend the heavenly parent of that brother or sister. I offend God.

What does God think of us when we kill or plan to kill his children? What would you think of me if I said, "John, you are a fine man," or "Mary, you are a good woman, but that brat of a son you have, I am going to kill him"?

You might answer, "Look, I might not be the best of parents, but stop that talk. That is my son you are talking about." God is better than any human parent. What does God think of us when we ask his help to kill his children?

This is the teaching underlying the command "Love one another." It is why Jesus can summarize our relation to God and to each other in the love-command.

It is the basic theology that opposes war. This is the rock on which the Christian who opposes war can stand. I may not know all of the intricacies of foreign policies or all of the complexities of military strategies. What I do know though is that there is only one God. We are all God's children. If foreign policy and military strategy cannot be reconciled with this belief, then I cannot accept them.

Jesus taught us to pray with the words "Our Father." Throughout his teaching he speaks of the Father's love for us. To deny that we are brothers and sisters to each other is a form of implicit atheism. We deny God's existence as our common source of being.

There is quite a difference between believing that all

humans are my brothers and sisters, and believing that some are and some are not. If I believe that some are not God's children, maybe I can kill them and please God; maybe I am better than they are because I am God's child and they are not. The bond between militarism and racism is evident here.

Prayer reflects belief. Prayer grows out of beliefs, and indicates what beliefs I hold. My prayer will be quite different when I believe we are all God's children, and when I do not.

For Christians who believe that Christ is our Brother, our relationship to each other as brother and sister is also an expression of our belief in and relation to Christ as our Brother and as God incarnate. Through the incarnation (God in human form), we are children of God because, if Jesus is our Brother, Jesus' Father is our Father too. Denial of our brotherhood/sisterhood is also an implicit denial of the incarnation.

Third Principle: The Almost Infinite
Value of the Human Person

The redemption of each person in Christ's blood gives each one an almost infinite value. Christ's death is not only a measure of God's love for us, but also a measure of our value in God's eyes—the death through crucifixion of his Son Jesus, that is our value. It is the Christian belief that God so loved each one of us that, if I was the only person in the universe, he would have given his life for me alone. The death of the Son of God on the cross is the cost of our salvation and the value of our individual worth. War denies all this with its depersonalization and its subordination of human life to the needs of the state, or to military necessity.

Fourth Principle: Means and Ends Relationship

The gospel teaches that there is an unbreakable internal relationship of harmony between the means we use and the end to which we aspire. The gospel teaches us that the goal of life is participation in the divine life. The means? Feed the hungry, clothe the naked, visit the prisoner, take in the homeless, bear one another's burdens along the journey of life. All these activities are compatible and harmonious, and in agreement with the end—participation in divine love.

This is all very familiar to us. In fact, even without faith we recognize the internal harmony between means and end in ordinary life. For example, I see a person driving around in a circle in a Washington parking lot. I ask, "Where are you going?"

"To Philadelphia!" he responds.

"But you will never get to Philadelphia riding around in circles."

"Yes, I will," he answers, continuing to drive in circles. So I conclude he is out of his mind: he cannot relate means and end.

In every aspect of daily life we recognize the necessity of means and end to correspond with each other. If I want to go upstairs, I raise my foot. If I wish to be healthy, I must eat. If a person cannot relate means to end, we consider that person insane. The story of a man who visited his friend in a mental hospital illustrates this. He found his friend constantly waving his right arm across and in front of himself.

"Why are you waving your arm, Bill?"

"To keep the elephants away."

"But there are no elephants around."

"Of course not, as long as I wave my arm," he replied.

To claim that war, even for a just cause, can be just irrespective of the means employed, is possible only on the assumption that the end justifies the means. To hold that military necessity knows no law, or that the end justifies the means, is a betrayal of Christian principle. "Nothing is more terrible," writes Jacques Maritain, "than to see evil barbarous means employed by men claiming to act in the name of Christian order. . . . The character of the end is already predetermined in the means. It is a truth inscribed in the very nature of things, that Christianity will recreate itself by Christian means, or it will perish completely."[2] This is quite opposite to the military method. There the means and end are contradictory. "Saving" is said to be done by killing and destroying.

The contradictions in military strategy are illustrated in the prayer at the christening of a nuclear submarine. "God bless this submarine! May it be an instrument of peace!" A submarine with nuclear weapons is seen as a means of peace. Even the act of using the term "christening" in launching a new warship is a kind of blasphemy. Christening is for people, and is a sign of God's grace.

Armies try to achieve peace through war, order through chaos, security through violence, the reign of law through lawlessness, to preserve honor by dishonorable acts. In the end they claim they save by destroying. This was actually voiced by the United States officer at Ben Tre, Vietnam, "We had to destroy the village in order to save it," he said.

Mark Twain understood that a prayer for victory is also a prayer that God will help us kill, make widows and orphans, and make our enemies hungry and homeless. In the words of Twain,[3] when we pray to God for victory, we pray to take the bodies of our enemy's soldiers and tear them "to bloody shreds with our shells." We pray to God to "help us to lay waste their humble homes with a hurricane of fire." We pray to God to "help us to turn them out roofless, with their little children to wander unfriended over the wastes of their desolated land."

When means and goal are separable and contradictory, the means tend to become the end as they do in Twain's prayer.

Gandhi said, "The creator has given us control . . . over means; none over the end. Realization of the goal is in exact proportion to that of the control of the means. This is a proposition that admits of no exception."[4]

In Jesus' teaching, means and ends are always compatible. "You will know them by their fruits. Are grapes gathered from thorns, or figs from thistles?"

When the means are not only incompatible with the goal, but contradictory to it, both reasons separate it from the gospel. The evil is not justified by the end envisaged.

The fruits of war are horror, death, suffering, moral degradation, arson, rape, lying, murder, and more war. There are things worse than war, and war brings every one of them with it.

War denies the everyday natural link between cause and effect. It teaches that there is a way of separating the effect from the cause. War denies the endless, changeless link of cause and effect. It says that a moral good (peace) can be obtained by an immoral means (killing).

It is not impossible to put means and ends together. We see an example of this in Mother Teresa of Calcutta. Interviewed on the BBC she was asked, "Mother Teresa, isn't it difficult for you to take care of the dying for twenty-five years? All those diseased, dying people?"

"No, not when you have faith."

"But, Mother Teresa, how do you keep faith going all those years?"

"When I hold the dying in my arms, I believe that I am holding Jesus."

There, you have complete identification of means and end. In loving my neighbor, I love God. All of us know people who in ordinary life live out their faith in God with their service of others.

Dorothy Day of the *Catholic Worker* said that there is no need of any special theology of peace. You just need to look at what the gospel asks and what war does. The gospel asks that we feed the hungry, give drink to the thirsty, clothe the naked, welcome the homeless, visit the prisoner, and perform the works of mercy. War does the opposite. It makes my neighbor hungry, thirsty, homeless, a prisoner, and sick. The gospel asks us to take up our cross. War asks us to lay the cross of suffering on others.

Jesus refused to establish his kingdom by means suggested by the devil, and contrary to his Father's plan. The devil asked him to prove that he was the Messiah by changing stones to bread, and by falling down from the top of the temple without being hurt. Both would be spectacular acts of power—far different from dying on the cross as a redemptive sacrifice. Jesus refused actions that were incompatible with his Father's plan for the Messiah. The devil promised him all the kingdoms of the earth if "bowing down, you will adore me." Jesus ordered Satan to "Be gone!" The means suggested by the devil were not compatible with his Father's plan, but contradictory to it.

Military means (killing and destroying) are a type of idolatry. It is worshiping a false god—Mars, the god of war. When we use military means, we trust in gods of metal, not in the living God. We do not trust in God's way of love, of redemptive suffering. We think we will get the peace that only God can give, without God's help and even in contradiction to God's plan. In fact, we think we will get peace with Satan's help and advice. We yield to the temptation that Christ rejected. We will do it our way. We will put our talents, our resources, our youth, our treasures, at the service of the god of war, not at the service of the God of love. The result that we get out of this is war. Our means and end are both compatible and convertible, on the side of war.

Fifth Principle: Imitation of Christ

The gospel teaches us that the best description of "holiness" is "imitation of Christ." Other descriptions like "doing God's will," "following the light," "being righteous," are all abstract compared to the "imitation of Christ." Unlike an abstract definition, Christ's life reaches us on every level: intellectual, physical, emotional, and spiritual. His life is not just words or a book. It is a living example.

Jesus was born in a stable, not a palace. He lived in a poor home, in a poor town, with poor parents. In his public life as a wandering street preacher, he said he had not a place to lay his head. He laid his head crowned with thorns on a cross, and he died a criminal, condemned by the religious community and the state.

We cannot seriously imagine Jesus pushing the button to launch a nuclear bomb, or registering for the draft, or wearing the uniform of any national state, or paying taxes for nuclear weapons, or working in a plant that manufactures weapons of death.

We, who know Jesus by faith, can be helped by the opinion of one who sees Jesus from outside the faith. During the Vietnam war a Catholic was appealing in court his claim to be a conscientious objector. At the beginning of the trial, the Catholic lawyer said, "Your honor, I know you are a Jew. You may be surprised to find a Catholic claiming to be a conscientious objector, because the Catholic Church is not known as a peace church."

"Just a minute, counselor," interrupted the judge, "It is true. I am a Jew, but I understand that this Jesus, whom you say founded your religion, was a Jew. He taught a doctrine of loving service to others. I have no trouble with people who say they are followers of this Jesus, and who refuse to take part in war. My trouble is with the big majority of those who call themselves followers of Jesus and accept war. Now you can go on with your case. You don't need to tell me about Jesus."

Any questions we might have about a text of Scripture (Does it approve war or not?) should be resolved by comparing it with the example of Christ's life. For example, "Render unto Caesar the things that are Caesar's." Does this mean that we should kill when Caesar says, "Kill"? Is it not clear from Jesus' life, and especially from his death, that even as Caesar killed him, Jesus would not defend himself? We need not imagine what Christ would do if asked to push the button that would send a nuclear weapon to kill millions. We have the example of his life. He was and is a pacifist—a peacemaker. He came to reconcile us to God (Eph. 2:12-19). Because of him we are no longer Jew and Gentile. We are one people. He has broken the barriers that separated us, and has reconciled us to God and to each other. He has done this by his death on the cross (Eph. 2:16).

Here we have the definition of peace. Peace is reconciliation between God, myself, and my neighbor. Peace is always three-sided: God, self, and neighbor. Peace can never leave God out. Nor can there be any peace with God and myself if I leave my neighbor out. Peace, like love, simultaneously includes God and neighbor.

For the Christian, Christ is the peacemaker, the reconciler. His method is the cross—accepting suffering with love, and not inflicting it onto others. The invitation of the gospel to love is entirely contradictory with the use of military force. Jesus wins love through suffering service. The military achieves its goal by force, fear, and death. Christ's way of life, Christ's example, was not the way of the military. It was a way of peacemaking, a way of making peace through the cross, through redemptive love.

Jesus' whole life showed the pattern of using peaceful noncoercive means to attain his end, the kingdom of God on earth. He chose poor fishermen as his apostles, not the great and powerful. He called himself the "good Shepherd," not a general. His Spirit appeared in the form of a dove, not a hawk or an eagle. His way of bringing peace was not the sword, not physical force, but rather, the appeal of a lover suffering for the beloved, accompanied by divine powers that transformed suffering and death into joy and life. The military system of getting your way through death and destruction leaves no room for the divine power that works through the paradox of saving life through losing your own, as exemplified in Christ's life and death.

His life is the "way" God teaches us to live. It is entirely opposed to the way of war. In three words he summarized all he taught and did, "Love your enemies."

CHAPTER TWO

New Testament Texts Used for War

One way to show that the New Testament does not approve of war is to examine the way texts have to be twisted to make them seem to support war. This is further evidence of the pacifist nature of the New Testament.

Pacifists are often accused of basing their belief on a single text, but as has been shown in the last chapter, the basic message that pervades the New Testament is pacifistic. Using single texts is a rather common practice with those who would like to have the New Testament approve of war. Here are some of these texts.

John 2:14-16

"In the temple he found those who were selling oxen and sheep and pigeons and the money-changers at their business. And making a whip of cords, he drove them all, with the sheep and oxen, out of the temple; and he poured out the coins of the money-changers and overturned their tables. And he told those who sold the pigeons, "Take these things away; you shall not make my Father's house a house of trade.""

Argument

I heard this text used as the basis of a sermon during

the Vietnam War: "Just as Jesus drove out the buyers and sellers, so are we in righteous anger, trying to drive out the communists, who attacked the poor people of South Vietnam. We are doing what Christ did."

Reply

This argument is ridiculous! Jesus didn't kill or threaten to kill others. A close look at the text makes it doubtful that he even used the whip on people. "He drove them all, with the sheep and oxen, out of the temple."

The fact that such an argument can be seriously used illustrates how difficult it is to find a gospel text that supports militarism.

From the context it is clear that Jesus' power was not his whip. Here in the temple the priests were in charge. They had their police at hand. The Romans had a garrison nearby and could have been called. Jesus' power was moral! His words and actions reminded them that they were violating their own laws. He had the support both of their law and of the people. They were afraid to oppose him because they were wrong and they knew it.

The outer court of the temple, which they had changed into a "den of thieves," was the only place where Gentiles were allowed for prayer. By closing it off from Gentile use, they were nationalizing the temple, including only the Jews. By his action Jesus was insisting that the temple be open to all—that it be an international place of prayer for all. This is the lesson he taught, a far cry from approval of war.

Matthew 26:52

"For all who take the sword will perish by the sword."

Argument

This text is sometimes used to approve defensive war. On the other hand, aggressive war, "taking the sword," will result in the death finally of those who are aggressors. Out of this comes the argument that defensive war is good and aggressive war is bad.

Reply

When Jesus says this in the Garden of Olives, he is about to be arrested by soldiers. Peter takes a sword to protect Jesus and cuts off the ear of a soldier. It is at this point that Jesus says, "Put your sword back into its place; for all who take the sword will perish by the sword" (Mt. 26:52).

Peter's action was the sword of defense, defending the very person of Jesus. Was there ever a more justified act of self-defense? But Jesus says, "Put your sword back into its place. . . . Do you think that I cannot appeal to my Father, and he will at once send me more than twelve legions of angels?"

Christian writers like Tertullian interpret this as a prohibition against military service. "Shall it be lawful to make an occupation of the sword when the Lord proclaims that he who uses the sword shall perish by the sword?" Far from supporting militarism, it clearly supports pacifism.

Matthew 10:34

"I have not come to bring peace, but a sword."

Argument

Jesus' kingdom will be established with the sword: so he approved of war.

Reply

A continuation of the text shows that the "sword" is the Word of God. "For I have come to set a man against his father, and a daughter against her mother, and a daughter-in-law against her mother-in-law; and a man's foes will be those of his own household" (Mt. 10:35-36). The Word of God reaches into conscience, and separates father from son, mother from daughter. In this way the Word of God, the Word of peace, is like a sword. For an example of this, consider what happened during the Vietnam War. Many a son told his father: "I believe God does not approve of this war, so I won't go." And many a father found himself in basic disagreement with his son on the war. The Word of God spreading through conscience can divide father and son like a sword.

Through the first three centuries Christians used this text to support their opposition to war. In fact "division" would be a better word to use than war. The same word "cut" or "divide" is used in Hebrews 4:12: "For the word of God is living and active, sharper than any two-edged sword, piercing to the division of soul and spirit, of joints and marrow, and discerning the thoughts and intentions of the heart."

More generally, the text shows how God deals directly, personally, with each one of us—how our faithful following of the Word of God will separate our paths from those who do not follow that path.

Matthew 8:5-13

"A centurion came forward to him, beseeching him and saying, 'Lord, my servant is lying paralyzed at home in terrible distress.' And he said to him, 'I will come and heal him.' But the centurion answered him, 'Lord, I am not worthy to have you come under my roof; but only say the word, and my servant will be healed. For I am a man under authority, with soldiers under me; and I say to one, "Go," and he goes, and to another, "Come," and he comes, and to my slave, "Do this," and he does it.' When Jesus heard him, he marveled and he said to those who followed him, 'Truly, I say to you, not even in Israel have I found such faith. I tell you, many will come from east and west and sit at table with Abraham, Isaac, and Jacob in the kingdom of heaven.... And to the centurion Jesus said, 'Go; be it done for you as you have believed.' And the servant was healed at that very moment."

Argument

Jesus praises a soldier. If war was wrong, Jesus would not praise a soldier, and then condemn war. By this praise of the soldier, Jesus approves of war.

Reply

Jesus approves of faith. He is not approving of the military profession. He marvels to find such faith in a Gentile.

The argument that Jesus does not condemn war is an argument from silence. Silence is always a weak argument. The point of the incident was to illustrate faith. Jesus praised Mary Magdalene's faith, but he did not approve of her practice of prostitution. Jesus praised the thief on the cross, but he did not praise his thievery.

Also war is not in question here. In Jesus' time the Roman soldiers were functioning as police in an occupied country.

Finally, Jesus did not come to condemn. He recognized splendid qualities to be found in individual soldiers, without approving the profession. Behind this is the belief that all can be redeemed.

Luke 11:21-22

"When a strong man, fully armed, guards his own palace, his goods are in peace."

Argument

True security consists in being armed to the teeth.

Reply

Read on further and you have the refutation. "But when one stronger than he assails him and overcomes him, he takes away his armor in which he trusted, and divides his spoil." The point is just the opposite of security through arms. It is rather the insecurity of arms—that military might is always vulnerable to the superior strength of a hostile enemy.

If Jesus' use of the example of armed strength constitutes approval of war, then it would follow that when Jesus uses the example of the end time coming like a thief, he approves of robbery.

John 15:13

"Greater love has no man than this, that a man lay down his life for his friends."

Argument

War is the supreme expression of love. This text is often used at the burial of a soldier who died in battle. The minister or priest often quotes this text and goes on to say something like this: "Our friend and brother, Private John, gave his life to save and defend all of us. As God rewards the martyrs who die for their faith, may God reward Private John who gave the supreme expression of love, his own life for the love of his friends."

Reply

Jesus didn't say, "He who kills his enemies for the sake of his friends shows love." The aim of the soldier is to kill the enemy. No soldier is told to go out and die, to put down his gun in resistance. Soldiers are taught to stay alive and kill. Generals don't ask their men to die. They order them to kill others. If they die trying to kill, it is twisting Christ's statement to say they "gave" their lives. There no doubt are cases where a soldier does die trying to save his endangered buddy. In such a case this text would apply, but it is the exception. Even the military calls such rescue work "action beyond the call of duty."

In today's nuclear army the whole emphasis is on security for ourselves and our nation; the emphasis is not on dying for others. The text does apply to the fireman whose regular duty calls on him to risk his life to save others. It does not apply to the soldier.

The essence of Christ's life was voluntary service to others (love). The conscript, or mercenary, is very far from imitating Christ. He kills because of government orders or because of the pay.

The cross of Christ rescued humankind; war has not rescued us. It is near blasphemy to appeal to the cross as the motive for war.

Luke 22:36-38

"He said to them, 'But now, let him who has a purse take it, and likewise a bag. And let him who has no sword sell his mantle and buy one. For I tell you that this scripture must be fulfilled in me, "And he was reckoned with transgressors"; for what is written about me has its fulfilment.' And they said, 'Look, Lord, here are two swords.' And he said to them, 'It is enough.' "

Argument

Jesus is no pacifist. He summons his followers to armed defense. He commands them all to buy swords. He gives express approval to their bearing arms, and, implicitly, he gives approval for using them.

Reply

This text is more difficult to understand than most. The literal interpretation favored by militarists conflicts with Jesus' follow-up statement. When they look around (as suggested by their statement, "Lord, here are two swords"), Jesus answers, "It is enough." But two swords were not enough for a war, or even for each of the disciples to have a sword!

The literal interpretation is in conflict with the whole context of the gospel and with Jesus' refusal, a few hours later, to be defended by the sword of Peter (Mt. 26:52). The literal interpretation conflicts with the way the apostles acted after Christ's death; and even with the traditional doctrine that makes murderous violence lawful for civil society but not for the church as church. Here Jesus is speaking to them as founders of the church.

A better interpretation is that Jesus was using figurative language. He was warning them that, when he died, a storm would break over them. He would not be around, so they would have to begin to look out for themselves. By commanding them to take a purse and a sword, he was warning them to prepare for a tragic spiritual battle.

When he realized that his disciples were taking his words literally, and were childishly presenting him with two swords, he says, "Enough," as though he were saying, "You don't know what I am talking about. Forget it. The Holy Spirit will take care of it later."

The obscurity of the text should be settled by the total gospel context, which is opposed to all murderous violence. It is a principle of sound biblical interpretation that an obscure text should be interpreted in accord with clear texts, if that is possible. The figurative interpretation makes that possible. Jesus, facing death, tries to warn them with a strong metaphor. They take it literally. He sees they don't understand and says, in effect, "Enough, let's go on to other things."

No twisting or turning of this text can equate Jesus' words with war. Carrying a sword on a journey in those days was not making war or preparing for it. It was a normal practice in areas beyond the cities to carry a sword as a protection against brigands and wild animals. Using a sword to kill others, however, was not in accord with the normal practice of Jesus' disciples.

An alternative interpretation of this Luke 22 passage is that it is a dramatic dialogue between Christ and his disciples on the use of violence. Jesus was testing how well his apostles had learned the lesson of the nonviolent, suffering nature of his messiahship. He had often told them he was going to be put to death; he had already reprimanded Peter for trying to make him change his mind on that point. Now he tells them again that he is going to accept being put to death.

He had told them all to travel without purse or staff or extra sandals; now he tests how well they understood the lessons, "When I sent you with no purse or bag or sandals, did you lack anything?" They said, "Nothing," "Now let him who has a purse take it and likewise a bag; and let him who has no sword sell his mantel and buy one." He doesn't say, "This is a test and I hope you are going to object because this is contrary to what I taught you before." They don't object. They take him seriously. "Here are two swords." They fail the test. They still have the wrong idea about his kingdom. They don't understand that violence is not the means that will establish the kingdom. He puts aside their comment on the swords with, "That is enough. Let's go."

This interpretation has Jesus saying something he doesn't usually mean. Did Jesus ever do this before? Yes. The same author, Luke 9, gives a parallel. When the crowd of five thousand were hungry he said to the disciples, "You give them something to eat!"

He knew the apostles didn't have bread to feed them. He wanted to get them to say, "You will have to do it. We can't." They passed that test, but on the use of violence, they failed.

More evidence for this "test" interpretation is found in the preceding verses of Luke 22 (which includes the Last Supper). The Supper itself, at which he had given his body and blood as food, was to be a memorial to his coming suffering and death. He washed their feet to show them how they should act.

As the apostles hear of his approaching suffering and death, they begin to argue about who will be the greatest in the kingdom. He tells them about the upside-down nature of power in the near kingdom. "The greatest among you will be the least" and he predicted the denial of Peter.

All this served as a summary of his teaching on the use

of power before he put them to the test.

The disciples failed. They didn't understand. At this point they did not identify themselves with the pacifist nature of Jesus' teaching.[5]

Mark 12:13-17
"Render to Caesar the things that are Caesar's, and to God the things that are God's."

Argument
Christ here tells us to obey the state in matters pertaining to the state, and war is one of those matters. In religious matters (worship, prayer, sacraments, personal moral questions), we should obey God. The sphere of God's demands are separate. They do not conflict with the state. War is the sphere of the state; so war is approved.

Reply
The context of this statement of Jesus shows that he was simply refusing to answer a hostile question that was meant to entrap him: "And they sent to him some of the Pharisees and some of the Herodians, to entrap him in his talk. And they came and said to him, 'Teacher, we know that you are true, and care for no man; for you do not regard the position of men, but truly teach the way of God. Is it lawful to pay taxes to Caesar, or not? Should we pay them or should we not?' But knowing their hypocrisy, he said to them, 'Why put me to the test? Bring me a coin and let me look at it.' And they brought one. And he said to them, 'Whose likeness and inscription is this?' They said to him, 'Caesar's.' Jesus said to them, 'Render to Caesar the things that are Caesar's, and to God the things

that are God's.' And they were amazed at him."

They marveled at him. He had clarified a muddy issue for them. Had he answered, "Submit to Rome," he would have lost some of his reputation with the people on whose necks Rome was then standing. Had he answered, "Refuse to pay," He would have gone to prison for inciting the people against Rome.

He not only escaped the dilemma, but by asking his questioners for the coin, (coins were not commonly used for exchange; barter was the typical method of exchange), he exposed them as owners of Roman coins—not something that would endear them to the crowd.

There is no reference here to war or even to paying taxes for war. Rather, Jesus implies, "Give Rome her pitiful coins, but give God the priority I have taught you to give. Seek first his kingdom and his righteousness, and all these things shall be yours as well" (Mt. 6:33). Not even our seeking of food and clothing should take precedence over seeking God. His parables on the kingdom of heaven show that it gets priority: like a pearl of great price or a treasure in a field for which everything else is sold. When he was asked what to do to gain eternal life, he replied, "You shall love the Lord your God with all your heart, and with all your soul, and with all your strength, and with all your mind; and your neighbor as yourself" (Lk. 10:27). There is no sign of second place for God, or for sharing first place with the state, in Jesus' teaching.

Dorothy Day of the *Catholic Worker* commented on the text from Matthew, "If we give God what is God's, there is nothing left for Caesar." This agrees with the priority that Jesus' teaching gives to serving God. It also coincides with the scriptural teaching of both Old and New Testaments that the entire universe is God's. The only claim the state can have on us is when it goes along with what God asks of us. The state has no authority separate from God, or in opposition to God, as the use of this text for militarism requires.

To take this text as supportive of the authority of the state would mean that Jesus was saying to the people of occupied Israel, "Render allegiance to the foreign tyrant (Rome). Do not take up arms to defend yourselves or to drive Rome out." This interpretation condemns militarism. I am not suggesting it as the best interpretation, but it is better than interpreting the text as support for war. The best interpretation is that the text has nothing at all to say about war. It is simply a refusal to answer a tricky question, a clever escape from a dilemma. This was also the way it was understood by his enemies, who accused him later of forbidding people to pay taxes.

Romans 13:1-7

The proof text for militarist theology has usually been Paul's call for submission to higher powers. Even though it is a bit long, it needs to be quoted in full:

"Let every person be subject to the governing authorities. For there is no authority except from God, and those authorities that exist have been instituted by God. Therefore he who resists the authorities, resists what God has appointed, and those who resist will incur judgment. For rulers are not a terror to good conduct, but to bad. Would you have no fear of him who is in authority? Then do what is good, and you will receive his approval, for he is God's servant for your good. But if you do wrong, be afraid, for he does not bear the sword in vain; he is the servant of God to execute his wrath on the wrongdoer. Therefore one must be subject, not only to avoid God's wrath, but also for the sake of conscience. For the same reason, you also pay taxes, for the authorities are ministers of God, attending to this very thing. Pay all of them their dues, taxes to whom taxes are due; revenue to whom revenue is due, respect to whom respect is due, honor to whom honor is due."

Often joined with this text of apostle Paul is this text of the apostle Peter (1 Pet. 2:13-17): "Be subject for the Lord's sake to every human institution, whether it be to the emperor as supreme, or to governors as sent by the emperor to punish those who do wrong and to praise those who do right. For it is God's will that by doing right you should put to silence the ignorance of foolish men. Live as free men, yet without using your freedom as a pretext for evil; but live as servants of God. Honor all men. Love the brotherhood. Fear God. Honor the emperor."

Argument

The apostle Paul is saying that we must obey those in authority, not only out of fear because they can hurt us, but we must obey for conscience' sake because all authority comes from God. In obeying them we obey God. The state is necessary and it is part of God's plan. When we obey state authority, we go along with God's plan. So when the government requires that we fight a war, God approves of our obedience.

Reply

Rather than approval of military power, a better interpretation of the Romans 13 text is that it approves of police power and civil law. There are many reasons for this interpretation.

(1) Paul speaks as a disciple of Jesus and as a Roman citizen.

He speaks as a disciple of Jesus, and he must be interpreted in the light of Jesus' life and Jesus' entire teaching. Paul is not preaching himself, but Jesus.

It may well be that Paul stresses obedience to the Roman government more than Jesus did. Paul was a Roman citizen. He saw the Roman roads as a means of promoting the Christian faith; they made communication easier.

(2) Was Paul saying Roman wars were moral?

He who proves too much, proves nothing. His words, "the bearing of the sword has its significance," proved too much, if used to support militarism. They would prove that the government of Rome, a government that had no thought of limiting the use of force to what Christians might consider moral, was acting as God wanted it to act. His words, taken as approving war, would have been a moral vindication of all the Roman soldiers had done. This is very unlikely.

Instead of that, he was implying, "They have the sword and will use it." He meant that it is not only foolish to forget this, but conscience allows obedience to many regulations of civil authority. Obedience to God does not mean rejection of all government authority, only that which contradicts God's law.

The time at which Paul spoke was a time in which the Roman government was enslaving and occupying Israel. This was the aggressive power that Paul asked to be obeyed. If ever a people had conditions for a just war, the Jews of Paul's day had them.

Because of this situation, if Paul was preaching

militarism, he certainly somewhere would have asked those who believed in Christ to cast off their Roman oppressors. But there is no trace of this in Paul. Paul says, "Obey higher powers." But does Paul mean by this, "Join the Roman army"? Does he mean that we should join today's army? A better interpretation is that Paul wished that Christians would avoid going out of their way to offend the Roman state as much as possible. Much of what civil law required (forbidding murder, theft, etc.) was also in accord with conscience. As Christians they would have enough trouble from the state without looking for it.

(3) Paul meant civil and police power, not military power.

Paul never refers to "war" in the entire text. "Higher powers" are the civil magistrates. "Sword" is the symbol of civil authority. A reasonable interpretation of the text is that the civil authority has the right to use a police force. This is in fact what the Roman government was doing at the time. Police power fits far better with the text of Paul than the mass killing that goes on in war. The words of Paul, "They carry out God's revenge by punishing wrongdoers," may possibly apply to the police force. It is difficult to see how this could apply to the killing of the innocent that is so much a part of war.

(4) Paul saw a need for civil government.

The entire passage of the apostle Paul is an apology for civil government, an effort to show the need for a system of civil government. But Paul makes it clear that government works through divine providence. However, the level of government and the order of government is different from the order of grace.

(5) Paul's message is best understood from a look at the Greek words he used.

Paul summarizes this in Romans 13:8-9. "Love one another; for he who loves his neighbor has fulfilled the law. . . . The commandments are summed up in this sentence, 'You shall love your neighbor as yourself.' "

Some light can be shed on Paul's meaning by a look at two Greek words used in Romans 13, "hupotasso" and "exousia." Paul chose to use "hupotasso," which means "be subject," rather than "obey." Paul was not prescribing blind obedience to the state but submission to it. He used three other words for "obey" in other texts.

"Exousia" is the word that Paul used for "powers." He viewed the governing powers as a part of God's original creation plan. God knew the need for order, cooperation, and direction in human relations. We call it the "authority of the state." "Powers" is a structure set up by God. The structure ("powers") is more than the sum of the parts.

Because of sin, the powers often fail to serve their order and function. They deify themselves, as in the Roman Empire. They demand unconditional loyalty and even worship. As part of fallen creation, Paul saw them as headed toward death. Survival became their goal, not good order. When their survival was threatened, the powers justified the taking of life for their own survival. Coercion, violence, and death became their normal way of life. They used the law as an instrument of sin and death (Rom. 8:2).

In Christ, love is the highest value system (1 Cor. 13:13). Violence and coercion play no part (Mt. 5:38-42). This view of creation and salvation leads Paul to tint all of creation, all of reality, with the hue of love. Thus, believers are called to love (agape) even the fallen, sinful powers. Paul exhorts Christians to love them as part of God's creation in the same way he asks love for all humans.

Paul's exhortations to unconditional love in Romans 12 and 13 are the context in which the five verses which seem to support war are set. He is asking Christians to submit to the ordering function of the powers. But submission does not lessen the priority of obedience to higher powers. For Christians, God deserves the highest allegiance. When the powers demand one thing and God demands another, believers should obey God (Acts 5:29). Conscientious objection to the powers occur, not to overthrow the powers, but to affirm their true vocation under God.

(6) Romans 13 should be read in the context of Romans 12.

In the last line of Romans 12, Paul says, "Do not be overcome by evil, but overcome evil with good." The state's alleged authority to kill and to ask others to kill is condemned by this text. Here the violence of the state, the killing done by the state, is the evil to be overcome by good. This statement of Paul is one of the most creative elements in the Christian ethic. Paul is here showing how it applies to the state. This is a pacifist attitude, not the attitude of a militarist.

The conclusion from Paul's text should be that as long as public authorities order what conscience approves, the Christian must submit to it.

(7) Early Christians on God and Caesar.
Earlier Christian writers believed that Scripture exalts

the claims of God above those of Caesar. All of them say, "We must obey God, rather than man."[6]

A general survey of the first three centuries shows that up until the third quarter of the second century (circa A.D. 170), the mainstream of Christian thought was consistently pacifist. After that time, signs of compromise with the pacifist ethic become increasingly evident. Yet the pacifist witness continues up to the fourth century.[7]

When Christian writers give their reasons for denouncing military service, the primary reason is faithfulness to Christ and to their baptism, and only secondarily, the concern for contamination with the Roman army and with false worship. Harnack, an authority on that age, says the objection to the army was that "it was a war-calling, and Christianity has absolutely renounced war and the shedding of blood."[8] Some characteristic statements that illustrate this are found in chapter three of this book.

These statements appear all the stronger when we remember that they were made by men for whom the Old Testament, with its frequent glorification of nationalism and militarism, was accepted as the Word of God, in the same sense as the New Testament was accepted. For those who might think that the pacifism of the gospel is useless and ineffective, it is interesting to reflect that the weak Christian pacifists of the first three centuries were able to live through and overcome the government of the Jewish priests, the government of Rome, and the religion of Rome. Most historians say that it was the opposition of the Christians, the willingness of the Christians to die for what they believed, that undermined the Roman Empire and contributed to its downfall.

It is quite certain that the tension between the ethics of

Christ and the ethics of the state, between Christ and Caesar, can never wholly be resolved. Both occupy a common field of action on which neither wishes to give way. A church, no less than the state, is committed to the belief that the life of a person finds its meaning and fulfillment only in a community of persons, free persons, united in a community. It is in relation to such a community that a church fulfills her mission. A church's witness can "be effective only as a continual challenge and criticism to the prevailing ideas and ways of life, insofar as these are contradictory to the Christian understanding of man's value and obligations. In a community, consciously committed to a contrary view, to the view that the state may take the life of a man or of other men when they decide, especially where the state has adapted a totalitarian policy, the Christian witness can be borne only at the cost of suffering and martyrdom."[9]

The problem of church and state resolves itself into the final question of where our loyalty lies; the conflict of loyalties can be resolved only in the old way, "We must obey God, rather than man" (Acts 5:29).

The Christian does not deny that civil authority comes from God. He or she affirms that there are certain government activities which the Christian conscience can never endorse. The Christian gives loyalty, where due, to Caesar, but recognizes that when the point is reached that a choice must be made between Caesar and Christ, he or she must follow Christ.

CHAPTER THREE

But Doesn't the Old Testament Allow Killing?

What about the wars of the Old Testament? There God is pictured as the God of hosts, leading his people in war—sometimes ordering them not to take prisoners, but to kill all who were captured. If it is clear in the New Testament that Jesus did not approve of wars, it is also clear that God, Yahweh, took part in wars in the Old Testament.

How, then, can war be forbidden? There are three ways the apparent contradiction between the Old and the New Testaments can be reconciled. First: we could postulate that there are two different Gods, one for the Old and one for the New Testament. Then there is no contradiction. But no believer in one God can accept this, so that is no solution. Second: we can take the New Testament as the interpreter, the fulfillment, the enlargement of the Old, and thus avoid a contradiction. Third: there is the theory of holy war based on God's covenant with his chosen people, a covenant that is superseded when the new covenant begins.

I will explain these last two views.

The New Testament Fulfills the Old
For the Christian who believes that God is the primary

53

inspiration of both the old and new dispensation and that God never changes, there must be some way of reconciling the pacifism of the New Testament with the wars of the Old Testament.

There are several ways of doing this. One is to understand how the New Testament is the fulfillment of the Old Testament.

In the Old Testament, murder is wrong; in the New Testament, even to think of murder or to be angry with your brother is condemned (Mt. 6:5). In the Old Testament adultery is wrong; in the New Testament, even to contemplate adultery is wrong.

Jesus put it this way, "You have heard that it was said, 'An eye for an eye and a tooth for a tooth.' But I say to you, Do not resist one who is evil" (Mt. 5:38). "You have heard that it was said, 'You shall love your neighbor and hate your enemy.' But I say to you, Love your enemies and pray for those who persecute you" (Mt. 5:43-44). Jesus fulfills and extends the law of Leviticus (Lev. 19:18) to include Gentiles and enemies—everyone.

This idea of extension or enlargement is a major element in understanding the relation of the New Testament to the Old Testament. In the New Testament there is no longer a selected group that is the chosen people; we are all God's people. The issue of slavery exemplifies this. In the Old Testament, perpetual slavery was allowed if the slave was an outsider, but not if he or she was an Israelite (Lev. 25:35-46). By enlarging the chosen group to include all humans, Jesus broke the institution of slavery.

The progression from the Old to the New Testament seems clearly a moral progression, a very positive step in the development of the emerging moral nature of all people.

How does this apply to war? Yahweh was involved in war in the Old Testament to raise and strengthen the faith, and to prepare for the coming of God's Son. With the coming of the Son, a worldwide community would begin, and the covenant relation with Israel would end. During the old covenant God required that the Israelites preserve their religious purity by not following outside religions, or marrying outside Israel. God would protect Israel, and even use her to punish the sins of others in war. Thus, God's people saw how they and all others were totally dependent on Yahweh.

During wars Yahweh showed Israel her dependence on him.[10] Once the Messiah came and the "chosen people" included all people, war was obsolete, and war was no longer a part of the covenant arrangement.

Christ came as the light of the world, and as Redeemer and Reconciler. It is in the light of Christ's life and teaching that believers in Christ should interpret the Old Testament, not the reverse. In the Old Testament God was dealing with a primitive human family, trying to arouse in them faith in the one true God. God allowed war as a means of stirring their faith by protecting and punishing them. When the Messiah came, there was no longer a "chosen people." We all became God's people. War, polygamy, slavery, and other concessions to human weaknesses were done away with.

Christians understand very well that the Jewish proscription against the eating of pork is no longer forbidden in the new law. Why is it, then, that we can't understand that God's use of war for evoking the faith of the chosen people is no longer God's way? Is it that we are hooked on war and want its imagined benefits?

If we believe there is only one God, who is the source

of truth in both Old and New Testaments, then we must find a reconciliation between the two. We cannot believe that the same God approves of war, then changes his mind in the New Testament and disapproves of war. To see the New Testament as fulfilling the Old Testament, and superseding the Old Testament, as I have outlined it, is one way of reconciling this apparent contradiction.

Holy War

The holy war developed out of the covenant God made with Israel. The covenant said in effect, "You keep my law—the Ten Commandments—and I will take care of you and protect you from your enemies." God himself would be their Lord, Leader, Protector. They would not be their own protectors; they would neither decide on war, nor the conditions under which, when ordered, it would be fought. This would be done by Yahweh. That was God's part of the covenant.

As long as the chosen people were faithful to these terms, God would protect them and assure their victory over their enemies. If they failed to fulfill any of the conditions (e.g., if they initiated a war on their own or violated conditions set down by Yahweh), they would go down in the dust of defeat.

A good example of all this was God's protection of the chosen people in Egypt as they were trapped on the banks of the Red Sea with Pharaoh's army rushing down on them. When the Israelites saw that the Egyptians were coming, they began to complain to Moses, "Is it because there are no graves in Egypt that you have taken us away to die in the wilderness? ... It would have been better for us to serve the Egyptians than to die in the wilderness" (Ex. 14:11-12).

Moses answered, "Fear not, stand firm, and see the salvation of the Lord, which he will work for you today; for the Egyptians whom you see today, you shall never see again. The Lord will fight for you, and you have only to be still." (Ex. 14:13-14). This message of Moses, "Be still and see the salvation of your God," summarizes God's relationship to the chosen people.

At God's command Moses stretched out his staff over the sea. The seas parted and the people of Israel marched through the walls of water to the right and left of them. When the Egyptians tried to follow, Moses, at God's command, stretched out his staff again over the sea, and the sea swallowed the Egyptians.

Was it any wonder that after that the people understood that their protection was in Yahweh?

This explanation seems important for understanding how much change the coming of the Messiah brought. We should not let ourselves get caught up in Old Testament wars so that we get lost in them. There is some danger of this even in reading about them. For that reason it is better to understand the New Testament on war, before trying to understand the holy war of the Old Testament.

Yahweh's leadership of Israel was symbolized in the holy of holies, the mercy seat, from between whose cherubim, the voice (but not the person) of God spoke: "The holy of holies is a throne room. The Israelites were a people with an empty throne, an invisible King."[11]

Even after the people clamored for and got a king, the kingship was limited in power. The prophets became the direct line by which God spoke to the king and to the nation. The king never was free to make war or to take life on his own authority. Nathan the prophet illustrates this.

He condemns the king for stealing another man's wife and taking the life of her husband.

If there was question of war, the prophet of Yahweh was to be consulted. The prophets would not only approve or disapprove the war, but would lay down the conditions under which it would be fought.

Wars in those days were generally waged for slaves and booty. So that Israel would know that any war in which God led them was not their war, but God's, they were forbidden to take slaves or booty. Sometimes this order included the direct command to kill all prisoners and all their animals.[12] Otherwise the prisoners might become slaves and the animals spoils of war. When the Israelites disobeyed these conditions (which they often did), they were punished by God, either by defeat in the war they attempted, or by invasion from their enemies.

The prophets Isaiah and Jeremiah exemplify this. Both prophets warned the Israelites not to oppose the enemies that were threatening. Isaiah warned against the Assyrians, and Jeremiah warned against the Babylonians. The Assyrians were not only an aggressive empire of conquerors for almost a hundred years, but they were quite candid about their use of brutality. Tablets that record their history carry recitals of their conquests and killings.

These tablets from the royal audience halls of the Assyrian capitals were read by foreign ambassadors who waited to see the great king. They would help soften them up for the interview. There was no question of justice on the side of the Assyrians; they were rapacious conquerors. Yet God used them to punish Israel.

Both Isaiah and Jeremiah had the job of telling Israel that for their sins, enemies would destroy them. They said, in effect, "Don't try to defend yourself. You don't deserve defense; you deserve punishment."

> "They have spoken falsely of the Lord and have said, 'He will do nothing; no evil will come upon us, nor shall we see sword or famine. The prophets will become wind; the word is not in them. Thus shall it be done to them.' " Therefore thus says the Lord, the God of Hosts: "Because they have spoken this word, behold, I am making my words in your mouth a fire, and this people as wood, and the fires shall devour them. Behold, I am bringing upon you a nation from afar, O house of Israel, says the Lord.
> "It is an enduring nation, it is an ancient nation, a nation whose language you do not know, nor can you understand what they say. Their quiver is like an open tomb. They are all mighty men. They shall eat up your harvest and your food. They shall eat up your sons and your daughters. They shall eat up your flocks and your herds. They shall eat up your vines and your fig trees; your fortified cities in which you trust. They shall destroy with the sword." Jeremiah 5:12-17.

For those who believed in armed resistance, there was every reason to oppose the Assyrians. Yet this was the empire of which Isaiah spoke, when he said to the king of Judah, "You must not fight the Assyrians." "Why not?" "Because they are the agents of God's vengeance on you. What you get is what you deserve, and it is a sin against God to resist."

The Just-Unjust War Theory of the Christian era is so far removed from giving God a decision in war that it never occurs to most Christians to ponder whether or not they deserve to be defeated; whether self-defense might be defense of an undeserving object. Both Isaiah and Jeremiah said that defense was for an unworthy cause. "You shouldn't even try to defend yourselves. You deserve punishment."

One point in favor of the Israelites, above every other nation, is that they usually had sense enough to repent, either in the midst of their punishment or after it. They turned to Yahweh and asked for mercy, and Yahweh always forgave them and helped them. They obeyed until they fell the next time. Unlike the Israelites, modern nations never repent; they just go on in their courses, until disaster finishes them.

A good example of conditions that Yahweh set up to let the people see that victory depended on Yahweh, and not on the strength of horse and chariot, is Yahweh's raising up of Gideon to rescue the people from the armies of Midian (Judg. 6:14). Gideon gathered together some of his followers, but Yahweh told him, "The people with you are too many for me to give the Midianites into their hand, lest Israel vaunt themselves against me, saying, "My own hand has delivered me" (Judg. 7:2). Yahweh ordered him to reduce the number of his soldiers.

All the fearful were ordered home. Then Yahweh told Gideon to take his men down to the waterside (Judg. 7:5-8). There Yahweh ordered Gideon to cut the number down to three hundred. "With the three hundred men ... I will deliver you, and give the Midianites into your hand," Yahweh said.

For seven years the Israelites had been under the heel of the Midianites. This was a punishment for displeasing Yahweh, so this rescue was no small event.

The number of the Midianites was past counting. "For whenever the Israelites put in seed, the Midianites and the Amalekites and the people of the East would come up and attack them; they would encamp against them and destroy the produce of the land, as far as the neighborhood of Gaza, and leave no sustenance in Israel, and no sheep or ox or ass. For they would come up with their cattle and their tents, coming like locusts for number; both they and their camels could not be counted; so that they wasted the land as they came in" (Judg. 6.3-4). This was the group that Gideon was called on to defeat with three hundred men. Gideon carefully followed Yahweh's instructions.

Gideon divided his three hundred men into three companies. To each he gave a horn and an empty pitcher, with a torch inside each pitcher. He said to them, "Look at me, and do likewise. When I come to the outskirts of the camp, do as I do. When I blow the trumpet, I and all who are with me, then blow the trumpets also on every side of the camp, and shout: 'For the Lord, and for Gideon' " (Judg. 7:17-18).

Gideon's soldiers obeyed his orders. "And the three companies blew the trumpets and broke the jars, holding in their left hands the torches, and in their right hands the trumpets to blow; and they cried, 'A sword for the Lord, and for Gideon!' They stood every man in his place round about the camp.... When they blew the three hundred trumpets, the Lord set every man's sword against his fellow and against all the army; and the army fled" (Judg. 7:20-22).

The victory was won with faith and trust in Yahweh. How far off this is from modern governments' way of acting. Imagine what an uproar there would be if a United States president announced that God had promised victory for the United States, provided we did away with our nuclear weapons, and fought only with horns, pitchers, and torches.

This was the way in which the holy war operated. The enemy and the conditions of the war were set by Yahweh so that there could be no doubt that victory was due to Yahweh, not to the strength of horse or chariot.

The Israelites were forbidden to make alliances or treaties with other nations. Their trust was to be in Yahweh alone.

Israelite leaders sometimes claimed that they acted in the name of Yahweh, when in fact they had no authority to do so. Once, after a defeat by the Philistines, the Israelites thought that by using the ark of the covenant as a rabbit's foot, a victory charm, they could win over their enemies. "Why has Yahweh allowed us to be defeated today by the Philistines? Let us fetch the ark of our God . . . so that it may come among us and rescue us from the power of our enemies" (1 Sam. 4:3, JB).

It didn't work. They were setting their own conditions without consulting the voice of Yahweh. In the battle they were defeated by the Philistines and the ark was captured.

Another example of the war made against the wishes of Yahweh occurred in the kingship of Ahab (1 Kings 22). King Ahab was considering making war. Many false prophets had already told him that Yahweh approved. The king knew that Micaiah was a prophet of Yahweh and sent for him. At first Micaiah said, "March and conquer." But when the King demanded that Micaiah speak the truth in the name of Yahweh, he said, "Yahweh has pronounced disaster on you." (v. 23, JB) For those words, one of the false prophets struck Micaiah on the jaw, and king Ahab said, " 'Seize Micaiah and hand him over to Amon, governor of the city. . . . Put this man in prison and feed him on nothing but bread and water until I come back safe and sound.' Micaiah said, 'If you come back safe and sound, Yahweh has not spoken through me' " (v. 28, JB). Ahab went into battle and was killed; the battle was lost.

Ahab did what was forbidden. He secularized war. He used war as an instrument of policy. He did this also by making treaties with other nations, depending on them instead of depending on Yahweh.

Another example is Solomon. Solomon built up an empire with forbidden alliances. In punishment God took the kingdom away from Solomon's son.

It should not surprise us that the Israelites, who did not have Jesus' example and teaching, should try to convince themselves that in some way or other the wars they planned by themselves had Yahweh's approval. Even after Christ's coming, many who believe in him follow a rationale for war that has no reference to Jesus or to his gospel. This is the Just-Unjust War Theory.

The Israelites had more excuse than we have. They had a history of God leading them and defending them in war. Christians never had this. We have a leader who died on the cross.

Old Testament Wars Are No Defense of Today's Wars

When we are tempted to use the Old Testament wars with their unrepeatable conditions as an argument for war today, we should answer the following questions:

Is there an identity between our Christian faith and the state? Religion and state were identified with each other in Israel but today they are separate.

In the absence of God's voice and of the prophets' warnings, how are we to determine who are God's enemies—on whom we will make war? Does the state on either or both sides of the conflict speak for God?

To which persons—to which leaders—will the voice of God speak saying when to fight and under what conditions? In the Old Testament God always determined when war was permissible, and what its conditions were.

Should whole populations be exterminated as in 1 Samuel 15? Will the newly married be allowed one year of married life before military service as in Deuteronomy 24:5?

If we find that the Old Testament authorizes modern war, does it not also authorize killing witches (Ex. 2:18)? owning slaves (Leviticus 25:44)? punishment by death of a rebellious, stubborn son? (Deut. 21:18-21).

The mere posing of these questions helps us see that the Old Testament is to be interpreted in the light of the New Testament, which is its fulfillment.

The God of battles, Lord of the heavenly hosts of the Old Testament, is also the Father of our Lord Jesus Christ. Jesus recognizes that all power and all punishment is in God's hands, not in human power. " 'Vengeance is mine,' says the Lord" (Deut. 32:35). So Jesus comes not as a Zealot, ready to kill his enemies. He is not a revolutionary like Che Gueverra or Camillo Torres.

When Jesus is moved to make a judgment on injustice, he spills his own blood. He identifies himself with both the victims and with the unjust oppressors. He drinks the cup of wrath for others. His Father, the Lord of hosts, has a justice that goes beyond human categories, the justice of God.

God Alone Is the Author of Life

With some understanding of how God used war to protect and punish his chosen people, we can reflect upon a deeper truth upon which the theory of holy war rests.

God, the Author of Life, has the power of life and death in his hands. God uses this power. God takes lives through the cataclysms of nature—through earthquakes, tidal waves, and volcanic eruptions. In the ordinary course of nature, God takes life through old age and through the natural process of disease.

In a word, life belongs to God. God does no wrong when God takes life. It is precisely because life belongs to God that God forbids humans to take it. When God directs humans to take life as God did in the Old Testament, the human, acting in obedience to God, is doing what is right. When Abraham prepared to take his son's life as God's command (Gen. 22:2), he was doing what was right. It was right because he was obeying God, and God has the ownership of life.

This is the truth that is rejected when humans take life. They take to themselves the role of God. They decide on life or death. They violate the command, "You shall not kill" (Ex. 20:13). "I am Yahweh your God who brought you out of the land of Egypt. . . . You shall have no gods except me" (Ex. 20:2-3, JB). This command forbids killing on human authority.

The state or the individual who takes life usurps God's place, and makes self or state into a false god. In both the Old and the New Testaments, there is only one true God who alone has the power of life and death. In the Old Testament God did order humans to kill, but with the New Testament, he no longer does.

Some say that they cannot believe in a God who takes life. Do they, then, believe that God gives life? that God alone is Creator? that all life is in God's hands? Do they believe that all life belongs to God? that life continues with God after this time of testing is over? These truths about conditions of life assert God's sovereignty over life. If we do not believe them, then we do not believe that there is a God.

Any claim that a state or an individual might make about the right to take life can rest only on a claim that God gave them the right. Such a claim is difficult to sustain in the light of God's use of war in the Old Testament, and God's ending of that use in the New Testament. Jesus summarizes it, "You have heard that it was said to the men of old, 'You shall not kill; and whoever kills shall be liable to judgment.' But I say to you that every one who is angry with his brother shall be liable to judgment; whoever insults his brother shall be liable to the council, and whoever says, 'You fool!' shall be liable to the hell of fire" (Mt. 5:21-22).

We Are Stewards of God's Creation

In the book of Genesis God tells us that all things on the earth are created for our use. We humans are appointed stewards over all creation to "replenish the earth" and "to subdue it" and "to have dominion over it."

As stewards we are not owners. We must render to God an account of our stewardship. Adam and Eve were driven out of the garden because they disobeyed God. They wanted to act independently, and not as his stewards.

The parables of the unjust steward, the talents, the laborers in the vineyard, the good servants rewarded—all repeat this theme of caring, responsible stewardship.

Any use or intent to use nuclear weapons violates this stewardship. Such weaponry will pollute the earth with radiation, will damage future generations with genetic disorders, and will cast in doubt even the very possibility of new birth and of new beginnings on planet Earth.

In both Genesis and in the parables, it is clear that God is the primary owner and Lord of all creation. At best, we are stewards to be rewarded according to our performance of stewardship.

Scientists participate in this stewardship responsibly as long as they use science to foster life. In this nuclear age, science has taken a turn toward death. As Robert Oppenheimer said when he learned of the devastation done by the Hiroshima bomb, "Scientists have known evil."

Pope John Paul II, talking to members of the Pontifical Institute for Science in 1983, said that scientists are responsible to see to it that science is not used for death and destruction.

Can any of us be part of the preparation for using nuclear weapons and still consider ourselves to be faithful stewards of planet Earth? There is much evidence for a negative response.

CHAPTER FOUR

The First Three
Centuries

The New Testament itself is evidence of first-century Christian belief in pacifism. The Gospels are the story of Jesus' way of life, a way of loving service, not a way of violence. They are in themselves primary first-century evidence of the Christian way of peacemaking.

A high percentage of Christians came out of the Jewish community. This community, especially in Judea, saw Roman imperialism at its worst: brutal, covetous, and totally lacking in consideration for local needs or customs. Non-Christian Jews revolted against Rome in a war of liberation, much like the revolt of blacks against South Africa, or Algerians against France. Christians knew about the revolt. Revolt leaders knew that the Christians did not side with the Romans, and actually sought Christian support, but violent, bloody revolution was not the Christian way. They refused to join.

Even the Christians who were in Jerusalem at the time the city was besieged (A.D. 66-70) refused to join the battle. This is good evidence that the central tradition of the early church was pacifist.

As the first three centuries moved on, one after another of the early Christian writers (known as the "Fathers" of the church) disapproved of Christians taking part in war.

If you were a young man during one of the first three centuries, you would not have known a single recognized leader in your church who would approve, much less advise, you to join the army. This is quite a change from the practice today when Christians advise their children to join the army for free education or to see the world. Early Christians disapproved of military life, not simply because the only army around was the Roman army run by a government busy persecuting Christians, or that Roman soldiers were obliged to take part in worship of false gods, including worship of the emperor himself. No! The basic reason Christian leaders disapproved was the commitment to Christ, made by the Christian at baptism. They found participation in war incompatible with following Christ.

A brief look at typical statements made by early church writers shows what advice a Christian would receive in those days if he thought of making a more secure life for himself by joining the Roman army.

Characteristic Statements of Early Christian Writers

Justin, a Christian martyr put to death by Marcus Aurelius in A.D. 165, wrote:

> We refrain from making war on our enemies ... for Caesar's soldiers possess nothing which they can lose more precious than their life, while our love goes out to that eternal life, which God will give us by his might.... (*The First Apology*, 39)

Justin quoted the Old Testament prophecy: "Nation shall not lift up sword against nation, neither shall they learn war any more" (Is. 2:4). Then he commented:

> You can be convinced that this has happened.... We who used to kill one another, do not make war on our enemies. We refuse to tell lies or deceive our inquisitors. We prefer to die acknowledging Christ. (*The First Apology*, 39)

> We, who were filled with war and mutual slaughter, and all wickedness, have each and all of us throughout the earth changed our instruments of war; our swords into ploughshares; our spears into farming tools, and cultivate piety, justice, love of mankind. (*Dialogue with Trypho*)

Here the prophecy of the Old Testament (Micah 4) is fulfilled:

> How could anyone accuse of murder and cannibalism, men who, as they well know, cannot bear to see a man killed—even if killed justly. We, thinking that to watch a man being killed is practically equivalent to taking life, refuse to attend the gladiatorial displays. (*An Embassy About Christians*, 35)

Other early Christian writers made similar statements. Clement of Alexandria (about A.D. 200) said that Christ "with his sword and with his blood gathers the army that sheds no blood."

"We are the race given over to peace" (*The Tutor*, 1, 12, 98).

"We have made use of only one instrument, the peaceful Word, with which we do honor to God" (*The Tutor* 4, 42).

Origen (A.D. 185-254) wrote:

> We Christians no longer take up sword against nation, nor do we learn to make war any more, having become children of peace for the sake of Jesus who is our leader.... And no one fights better for the King than we do. We do not indeed fight under him, although he require

it, but we fight on his behalf, forming a special army, an army of piety, offering our prayers to God. (*Against Celsus, 8, 73*)

To those who ask us where we have come from, or who is our commander, we say that we have come in accordance with the counsels of Jesus, to cut down our warlike and arrogant swords of dispute into plowshares, and we convert into sickles the spears we formerly used in fighting. For we no longer take sword against a nation, nor do we learn any more to make war, having become sons of peace for the sake of Jesus, who is our Commander. (*Against Celsus* 5, 33)

These thoughts were typical of the preaching and writing in the first three centuries of the Christian church. The young man who might be thinking about joining the army would hear this not only at the eucharistic celebrations, but if it was a time of persecution, he would know friends and every family who suffered for their faith at the hands of Roman soldiers. Joining the army would mean not only going against the gospel, but it would also mean deserting friends and loved ones who were living victims of that same army, offering their eucharistic celebrations, and burying their martyred dead in underground cemeteries to escape the persecutors. These personal statements probably appealed to the young men who lived in the age of the martyrs more than rational arguments did. How could they look for an easy life when their families and friends and those who shared their faith were forced to live underground? They might have argued that they could do more for their friends if they were in the Roman army. But would their families and friends want them to join?

Also, if they got to the point of asking themselves if their faith allowed it, they could not find a single well-known writer or teacher of the age who said "Yes." As the years rolled by, however, the number who said "No" continued to increase.

Over the first centuries the leaders of the church, who included saints and martyrs, presented an almost unanimous attitude of opposition to killing in war.

Here are some of the more prominent, with some of their typical statements.

Tertullian (c. A.D. 160-220) writes:

> Shall it be lawful to make an occupation of the sword, when the Lord proclaims that he who uses the sword shall perish by the sword? And shall the son of peace take part in battle when it does not become him, even to sue at law?... The very act of transferring one's name from the camp of light to the camp of darkness is a transgression. Of course, the case is different, if the faith comes subsequently to any who are already occupied in military service, as with those whom John admitted to baptism, and with the most believing centurion Christ approves, and whom Peter instructs. All the same, when faith has been accepted and sealed, either the service must be left at once, as has been done by many, or else recourse must be had to all sorts of quibbling, so that nothing may be committed against God.... Do leaves make up the laurel of triumph—or do corpses? Is it decorated with ribbons or tombs? Is it besmeared with ointments or with the tears of wives and mothers—perhaps of some even who are Christians—for Christ is among the barbarians as well? (*On the Garland II, 2*)
>
> "How shall a Christian wage war? Nay, how shall he even be a soldier in peacetime without the sword, which the Lord had taken away? For although soldiers had come to John, and had received the formula of their rule; although even a centurion had believed, the Lord afterwards, in disarming Peter, ungirded every soldier. (*On Idolatry,* 19)

Cyprian (248-258), a bishop and a canonized saint, wrote, protesting against the dual standard of morality which brings it about, that "if murder is committed privately, it is a crime. But if it happens with state authority, courage is the name for it" (*Letters*, 1, 6).

"Adultery, deceit, and the taking of life are mortal sins ... after partaking of the eucharist the hand is not stained with blood and with the sword" (*On the Value of Patience*, 14).

Later, Lactantius wrote at the beginning of the fourth century:

> It will not be lawful for a just man to serve as a soldier, for justice itself is his military service; nor to accuse anyone of the capital offense, because it makes no difference whether you kill with the sword or with the word, since killing itself is forbidden. And so, in this commandment of God, no exception at all ought to be made to the rule that it is always wrong to kill a man whom God had wished to be regarded as a sacrosanct creature.

More writers of the first three centuries are quoted by John Ferguson in *Politics of Love*, by Roland H. Bainton in *Christian Attitudes Toward War and Peace*, and in *The New Testament Basis of Pacifism* by G. H. C. Macgregor. Bainton says, "All of the outstanding writers of the East and the West repudiated participation in warfare for Christians."[13] This does not mean that there were never any Christians in the army during the first three centuries. But it does mean that pacifism was the dominant pattern in the early church. This has special significance for a church like the Catholic Church in which tradition is as important a source of truth as revelation. It means too that to be traditional in Christian sense is to be pacifistic.

Most commentators on this early history, like Bainton and Leclerc, are impressed by the amount of literature denouncing warfare and bloodshed. Some, like Edward Ryan, S.J., writing in *Woodstock Letters,* found an argument against Christian pacifism in the silence of Church Council decrees against militarism during this period. He argues that the Church Councils didn't define "anything in the way of pacifism as church teaching." This is an argument from silence which is very weak as a conjecture. It is not at all likely that a Church Council would speak out on a problem that hardly existed. There were enough pressing problems without that.

Councils generally act when there is serious need— when people are going astray and need to be called back to truth that is being ignored. There was no such need in the first three centuries.

Besides, why openly defy a government that is already persecuting you when your actions speak for you?

John Ferguson makes a good parallel between Christians during those first three centuries and the followers of Mahatma Gandhi. Gandhi, who died in 1948, taught pacifism. Suppose Gandhi died when Christ did. Suppose "that no follower of Gandhi was to be found in the army before the year A.D. 100, and very few, before the year 250. We might think Gandhi's pacifism of quite extraordinary power. If there was change between 250 and 350, we should attribute it, rather sadly, to a falling away from a basic commitment."[14]

If disciples of Gandhi lived that way for that long, it would surely be a good argument that Gandhi taught pacifism. Likewise, the way early Christians lived shows that they believed that Christ taught pacifism.

The absence of Christian soldiers in the army is more evidence. For the first 150 years, there is no record of Christian soldiers in the Roman army. Until A.D. 300 the number is very few. Even at the beginning of the fourth century, emperors Diocletian and Galerius purged their armies of the few Christians (a sign that the number of Christians in the armies was small).

A church order from Egypt reads, "A catechumen or believer, who wishes to become a soldier, shall be rejected because it is far from God" (Statute 29). Another statute (28) reads, "They shall not receive into the church one of the emperor's soldiers. If they have received him, he shall refuse to kill, if commanded to do so. If he does not refrain, he shall be rejected."[15]

Saint Maximillian was one of the first draft resisters. In the year 295 he was executed for refusing military service. His fellow Christians considered Maximillian a model for all Christians and preserved a record of his trial.

In the year 295 on the 12th of March, at Theveste in North Africa, the conscript Maximillian, with Victor his father, was brought into the court of Dion the Proconsul. Valerian Quintian, the imperial commissioner, was present.

The attorney for the treasury, Pomeianus, spoke first: "As Maximillian is liable for military service, I request that his height be measured."

Dion, the proconsul, said to Maximillian, "What is your name?"

Maximillian: "Why do you want to know my name? I am not allowed to be a soldier. I am a Christian."

Dion: "Measure him."

When this was done, the assistant announced, "Five feet, ten inches."

Dion: "Put the badge on him."

Maximillian resisted saying, "I refuse. I cannot serve."

Dion: "Be a soldier. Otherwise, you must die."

Maximillian: "I will not be a soldier. You can cut my head off, but I will not be a soldier of this world. I am a soldier of my God."

Dion: "Who has put these ideas in your head?"

Maximillian: "My conscience and he who has called me."

Dion said to the young man's father: "Give him some good advice."

Victor: "He is old enough. He knows what he has to do."

Dion to Maximillian: "Be a soldier, and accept the badge of enlistment."

Maximillian: "I have nothing to do with your badge. I already bear the sign of Christ my God."

Dion: "I am going to send you to join your Christ, here and now."

Maximillian: "Then do so quickly. It would be a great honor for me."

Dion: "Become a soldier, and take the badge. If not, you will die a shameful death."

Maximillian: "I shall not die. My name is already written down with my God. I cannot be a soldier."

Dion: "Think of your youth and become a soldier. It is a fine life for a young man."

Maximillian: "My service is to my God. I cannot be a soldier for this world. I have already told you. I am a Christian."

Dion: "In the bodyguards of our lords, Diocletian and Maximian and Constantius and Maximus, there are Christian soldiers and they serve."

Maximillian: "They know what they have to do. But I am a Christian and I cannot do what is evil."

Dion: "But those who serve—what wrong do they do?"

Maximillian: "You know very well what they do."

Dion: "Be a soldier. By refusing, you are inviting a cruel death."

Maximillian: "But I will not cease to exist. If I leave the world, I shall live with Christ, my God."

Dion: "Strike his name off." When this was done, he said to Maximillian: "Since you have insubordinately refused to serve in the army, you shall suffer the penalty of the law. Let this be an example to others." And from a tablet he read out his sentence: "Maximillian, out of insubordination, has refused the military oath, and is, therefore, condemned to die by the sword."

Maximillian: "God be praised."

He was twenty-one years old, three months and eighteen days. [16]

The spirit of the age comes through in this scene. It is the spirit of a man who knew he had the backing of his family and his church. His example is so strong that it even encouraged young men in the United States who refused to kill in the Vietnam War. Draft counselors used the story of Maximillian to encourage young American Christians to resist military service.

What must have been the impact of his death on those who knew him, and believed with him, centuries ago!

Pope Damascus' inscription on the grave of two soldier martyrs expresses some of the glory of being a pacifist in those early days. He writes:

They had signed up for soldiery, undertaking cruel duties. Together they watched their overlord's commands,

> ready to do his bidding at the spur of fear. A miracle of
> faith! All at once, they laid aside their madness. They
> turned. They fled. They abandoned the general's godless
> camp. They threw down their shields, their helmets, and
> their blood-smeared swords. They rejoiced to acknowledge
> and bear along Christ's triumphs.

This is a deeply moving example of strong faith!

The change away from a strong commitment to pacifism came with Constantine. It was not sudden, but had been building up gradually. Christians were more numerous, more organized, and more centralized. This had something to do with it. Time and the wearing effect of persecution had an influence. The general weakening of Rome, and the need of Christian support against outside enemies was an element.

Constantine himself was a catalyst. He did not become a Christian until he was on his deathbed. In A.D. 312 he attributed his military victory to the sign of the cross that he saw in the sky. He was a believer in the sun as a god, and may have found the cross woven into the sun's rays. At any rate, he ended the persecution, and gave privileges to Christians. He made it possible to become honorable in Caesar's eyes and also to be a Christian. This was something new!

This was a big change. With it the Christian attitude toward war shifted. No longer was the state the persecutor or the enemy. Now it was a friend, and soon it was a friend in need of Christian soldiers. The blessings that came to the persecuted ceased coming to many Christians. They yielded to Caesar's temptations and joined in Caesar's wars. The mechanism by which this was done was the Just War Theory or, in other words, the Just-Unjust War Theory.

Nonetheless, the witness to pacifism continued through the centuries. Not only are their individual witnesses like St. Francis of Assisi, Erasmus, Tolstoy, George Fox, William Penn, Gandhi, and Martin Luther King, but also, whole groups of such Christians. Throughout the centuries they have kept alive the corporate Christian witness to their belief in the gospel as a way of peace that excludes war.

The Waldensians of the later Middle Ages, the sixteenth-century Anabaptists led by Menno Simons—a Catholic priest who founded the modern Mennonites, the Church of the Brethren, and the Quakers—these are all examples of witness to Christian pacifism. These last three groups are active in the United States, and have had an effect on national policy, which is surprising in light of their small size. All three groups together number about three million, worldwide, with about half of them in the United States, drawn here by the hope of religious freedom. Their stand against conscription led to the adoption into the U.S. Selective Service law of clauses, allowing for conscientious objection to those "opposed to war in any form." The importance of their continued and corporate Christian witness to the gospel of peace was more understood by the mainline Christian churches, when the nuclear age dawned. Weapons of massive destructive capacity began to make many Christians take a fresh look at war and at the gospel of peace.

Statements from Vatican Council II, condemning the destruction of whole areas with their people as "contrary to every law, human and divine" (sec. 80, *Church in the Modern World*), are an appeal to conscience. The document calls on persons in the armed forces not to obey blindly, but to weigh the morality of the orders they follow (sec. 8); and it suggests that nonviolence is a better way of following the gospel (sec. 78). The National Council of Churches and individual Protestant groups have made similar statements.

All of this, plus an understanding of nuclear technology and its terrible dangers, have turned the thoughts of many back to a new appreciation of the faith and pacifism of the first three centuries, and away from the Just War Theory, or what I always refer to as the Just-Unjust War Theory.

CHAPTER FIVE

The Just-Unjust War Theory

With the accession of Constantine to power, the church as a whole gave up her anti-military leanings, abandoned all her pacifist scruples, and finally adopted the imperial point of view, says Cecil Cadeaux in *The Church in the First Centuries*. Even if the change was not that drastic, a new emphasis is evident among the leading Christian writers after the third century. Athanasius claimed it is praiseworthy to kill enemies in war. Ambrose, Augustine's teacher, agreed. Augustine defended the position with detailed arguments.

The war question was settled, not on theological merits, but on a combination of circumstances, Cadeaux concludes. The joy of Constantine's deliverance was so great that it caught the church off guard. Christians had no part in Constantine's decision, so the problem of what was happening dawned on the Christian mind only in a fragmentary way by slow degrees. A church that was drenched in the blood of hundreds of her martyrs had shown that she was strong and even grew stronger under persecution. Such a church could have opposed even Constantine if its mind had been set about war being absolutely and always opposed to the gospel. But the mind of the Christian church was unclear by this time.

Besides, church doctrine on peace or war had never been defined. The church had an aversion for bloodshed and it practiced pacifism. Yet it had no doctrinal or theological definition of its attitudes. Now by default it began to shift into a practice of accepting war. The shift was hastened and strengthened by Augustine's formulation of the Just-Unjust War Theory.

This fourth-century theory is worth looking at because it is the lever that separated Christian theory from practice, and has helped to maintain the separation over the centuries. Apart from pacifism, it is the only other theory Christians have ever had that tried to relate Christian faith to war and peace.

Augustine formulated it like this: In general war is wrong; war is contrary to the gospel of peace. But there may be conditions under which war may not be a violation of the gospel, but may be an act of mercy and love. When these conditions are faithfully fulfilled during the entire war, then the war is not morally wrong.

Conditions of the Just-Unjust War Theory

The Just-Unjust War Theory maintains there are at least these five criteria by which a war can be judged just:
1. Declaration of war must be made by the king.
2. War must be the last resort.
3. A good intention must guide the side declaring war.
4. The war must allow for the protection of the innocent.
5. A proportion of good over evil must be kept.

The following is a general explanation of each condition of the theory.

1. Declaration of war by the king

There were no national states in Augustine's day. In today's world of national states, the equivalent of king would be the supreme political authority. In the U.S. this would mean a declaration by Congress.

An undeclared war would be the misuse of authority and a threat to the innocent, inasmuch as they might be caught unawares. Use of nuclear missiles before declaring war would violate this condition.

2. War as a last resort

Every other means of solving a conflict must be tried before war is declared. Every effort of reconciliation must be made such as arbitration and negotiation. Today that would certainly mean bringing the conflict to the United Nations for discussion and decision. In the Middle Ages, between Catholic kings, it would have included asking the pope to act as a mediator.

3. Intention

The intention of declaring would have to be the restoration of justice: the king would be acting as vicar for the human family seeking to restore or preserve justice. The intention could never be a national state seeking its own benefit. The intention could not be land grabbing, economic control, or domination.

"Good intention" as used in this theory is not some vague whimsical notion. As interpreted by its authors and supporters, it means:

(a) That you have a just cause. "Just cause" means these two features exist: moral guilt is on one side and there is a sure, conscious knowledge of that guilt. How difficult this is becomes clear when you try to find an example of it in real life. There are no clear examples. For instance, imagine that nation A invades nation B in order to get land. In doing this, nation "A" is conscious that what it is doing is morally wrong. There must be no doubt about this consciousness of wrongdoing. This must be clear before nation B would have a just cause for war against nation A.

(b) No war can be just that includes a desire to harm, a lust for power, or for revenge. None of these are good intentions. Slogans like "Remember the Maine" or "Remember Pearl Harbor" are alien to the Just-Unjust War Theory.

(c) In no war are both parties in the right. One side is always unjust. They can't both have the "good" intention required.

4. Protection of the innocent

The direct taking of innocent lives is never allowed. No cause is great enough to justify that. This condition limits direct killing in war to killing only the guilty. Conscripted soldiers are innocent, like civilians. Only volunteer soldiers are considered guilty in a just war.

Only "indirectly" is the way that the innocent can be killed, so that their death is not intended, but is a side effect of the necessary killing of the unjust enemy (for example, the destruction of a building full of enemy soldiers, in which there are also a few innocent noncombatants). How many innocents might be allowed to be killed as a side effect of killing the soldiers leads to the next principle.

5. Proportionality

This principle means there has to be a balance between the evil done and the good hoped for—a balance favoring the good. For example, to destroy a building with one hundred enemy soldiers and two innocent children would be allowed. If conditions were reversed, and two soldiers were among ninety-eight innocent, there would be no justifiable proportion. This principle would exclude killing where there were fifty innocent and fifty guilty. There would be no favorable proportion.

Even a superficial reflection upon these conditions raises doubts about how they could ever be fulfilled. Yet these are the conditions that have to be fulfilled every day of a war to make a war "legitimate." As long as all of these conditions are completely fulfilled, war, according to this theory, is considered just. The defect of any one of these conditions, at any time in a war, would make it unjust, according to the theory.

The question of the difficulty of getting all these conditions together and operating throughout a war, and the opportunity for endless argument about whether certain conditions are fulfilled, indicates some of the weakness of the Just-Unjust War Theory.

Weaknesses of the Just-Unjust War Theory

Even before getting into particular weaknesses of the theory, it must be noted that there is a debate whether these five conditions constitute *the* Just War Theory. Leroy Walters in *Five Classic Just-War Theories*[17] argues that there is no one Just War Theory, but five different theories by five main supporters: St. Thomas Aquinas, Suarez, Vitoria, Grotius, and Gentili. With Augustine there is a sixth.

Theorists differ on the number and content of conditions required. Some, like Aquinas, include proportion and care of the innocent under the heading "just cause." Others, like Franciscus Stratmann, O.P., who led the

Catholic peace movement in Germany after World War I, refined the conditions and enlarged them into ten conditions.[18]

Which theory is correct? Which should I follow? This kind of an argument could go on forever and most likely will. What good is a theory whose very statement is not agreed on by those who support it? The war would be over before the argument was ended.

It reminds me of the seminarian who was trying to get a faculty member to go with a group to the White House to protest Nixon's forty-five days of bombing of Cambodia. The faculty member kept delaying, asking for more time to think about it. Finally, the seminarian asked in disgust: "Will you come with us to demand that Nixon extend the bombing long enough for you to make up your mind?"

Aside from the debate as to which Just War Theory to follow, the five criteria outlined above themselves have weaknesses.

1. Declaration of war by the king (or top political leaders) presents a special difficulty for us in the missile age. Missiles can travel between Moscow and Washington in twenty-four minutes. That doesn't allow Congress time to declare war or time to respond. Then, the response may be so massive that it will kill millions and create much more killing than most wars in history. Even if Congress authorizes the president to use massive response, this condition of the Just-Unjust War Theory is not really fulfilled because it is doubtful that Congress has power to delegate the power to declare war to the President. Japan's attack on Pearl Harbor before a declaration of war violated this condition, as did Hitler's attack on Poland.

Of course, first use of nuclear weapons, which presidents Ford, Carter, and Reagan have accepted as U.S. policy, would violate this condition. Even *intent* to use first strike capability is a violation. Development of first-strike weapons like the Trident submarine and the cruise missiles is a part of that intent. These weapons are aimed at enemy silos (weapon sites). The highly maneuverable accuracy of these weapons would not be needed, if we were aiming to defend ourselves after being hit. The silos would presumably be empty before we fired if we had already been attacked.

2. Protection of the innocent is a condition which would certainly be violated by any use of nuclear weapons on cities. Such use would also come under the condemnation of Vatican II, which forbids the use of weapons of massive destruction on whole areas and their population (*Church in the Modern World*, sec. 80).

Since the use of nuclear weapons would very likely escalate to the point of killing whole populations, any use of nuclear weapons would probably violate this condition. Therefore, nuclear weapons cannot be used at all. In matters of life and death, probability cannot be used for one side of an argument. Certainty is required. Likewise, the use of conventional weapons by a nuclear power risks nuclear war with its destruction of millions of innocent victims. Taking such a risk violates the "protection of the innocent" condition of the Just-Unjust War Theory.

3. Proportionality is a condition which undermines the theory in a nuclear age. In *Nuclear Disaster*, Tom Stonier estimates that if one twenty-megaton weapon were detonated in central New York City, seven million people would die from the blast and the resultant firestorm and radiation. President Kennedy estimated that any large-

scale exchange between the U.S., and another nuclear power would result in 80,000,000 American deaths, and almost double that in enemy deaths.

In 1974-1975, the annual report of the American Academy of Science said that a large scale nuclear exchange between the U.S. and USSR would probably kill all human life on earth because the ozone layer would be damaged to such an extent that the lethal ultraviolet rays of the sun would cause blindness and finally destroy the food chain that sustains life. If this happened, it would lead to extinction of the human species.

In a summary of his book, *Fate of the Earth* (see bibliography), printed in the *Congressional Record* (1982) by Senator Alan Cranston, Schell says: "There are some 60,000 nuclear warheads in the world. They are a nemesis of all human intentions, action, and hopes—culminating in an absolute and eternal darkness in which no nation, nor society, nor ideology, nor civilization will remain; in which never again will a child be born; in which never again will human beings appear on the earth, and there will be no one to remember that they ever did."

On leaving office in 1980, President Carter said that in one minute of an exchange between the U.S. and USSR more explosive power would be unleashed than all that was dropped on Europe and Japan by the Allies during World War II.

Carl Sagan, astronomer from Cornell, predicts that a "nuclear winter" would follow an exchange of one fifth of the world's nuclear arsenal. The dust sucked up into the stratosphere by the mushroom clouds would be enough to shut out the sun's sunlight so that the temperature on earth would go below freezing and cause deaths by starvation.

The Physicians for Social Responsibility say that only a very small percentage of those millions needing medical care during a nuclear exchange will receive it because doctors will be dead, hospitals ruined, transportation destroyed, and medications ruined. They conclude that "preventive medicine" dictates that they speak out ahead of time and warn the public, according to their president Dr. Helen Caldicott, not to expect any medical help during a nuclear war, for there won't be any.

The Council of the Federation of Concerned Scientists wrote an editorial in their *F.A.S. Public Interest Report* (Feb. 1981) which said that if the enormous explosive power that we have in our stockpiles were ever used, the consequences in terms of human casualties and physical destruction would be virtually incomprehensible.

Because of the enormous destructive capacity of our weapons, both the USSR and the U.S. would be destroyed as viable societies in a nuclear war. No one would win. This situation rules out the possibility of fulfilling the requirement of proportionality.

This condition by itself seems sufficient to invalidate the Just-Unjust War Theory in a nuclear age. As Pope John XXIII said, "No intelligent person could think of the use of nuclear weapons as a way of restoring justice" (*Pacem in Terris*).

How is the ordinary person to know for sure when this condition is fulfilled? To apply it, one must know for certain just how much killing, destroying, damaging of innocent and combatants, is being done every day of the war. Where is the average soldier, or civilian, to get such information reliably during time of war?

Consider Vietnam! In 1968 during the war the U.S. Catholic Bishops asked in a public statement, "Have we already reached or passed the point where the principle of proportionality becomes decisive? How much more of our resources in men and money should we commit to this struggle? Has the conflict in Vietnam provoked inhuman dimensions of suffering? Would not an untimely withdrawal be equally disastrous?" Here the war has been underway for years, and the bishops merely raise questions. They don't answer them. If they can't or won't, how is the ordinary individual supposed to answer them?

We learned the truth about the Vietnam War from the Pentagon Papers—how the U.S. government deliberately deceived not only the public but even the Congress. Yet this theory presupposes that the soldier must know the truth about a war and make ethical judgments based on that knowledge.

4. The theory never worked in practice. From the time of its formulation until the present, there is no record of any nation using it or of any war having been avoided by it. Even after wars were over no Conference of Bishops ever condemned any war on the basis of this theory— neither their own war, nor the war of any enemy nation.

5. The theory presupposes the very thing it is supposed to prove: that some killing is allowed on human authority.

6. Intention assumes that in war one side will be just and the other unjust. This never happens. Instead, both sides claim they are right and kill each other—often in God's name.

7. The theory was formulated to show that *some* wars might be an exception to the law of the gospel. Instead, it has become a theory used to justify every war that comes along. Instead of justifying an exceptional war, it is used to make all war acceptable.

8. The theory allows each nation to judge its own cause. This violates the common-sense adage that no one is a good judge in his own case.

9. How could you ever know enough of the intent and actions of governments to make a sure judgment about participating in a war declared by your own country? Yet according to traditional morality, one may not act, even on probability, where human life is concerned.

10. This complex theory nullifies the simple gospel message of love, a message meant for all and understandable by all. The theory is so complex that it is beyond the reach of the ordinary person.

11. The theory is unsuited to the age of total war and nuclear technology. The U.S. Catholic Bishops' Pastoral on peace (God's Challenge and Our Response, May 3, 1983) says that use of nuclear weapons makes it impossible to protect the innocent or accomplish any good proportionate to the evil.

12. The theory is stretched to include almost anything. One advocate of the theory says that it allows torture of prisoners and that noncombatants may be killed. Another advocate, Archbishop Phillip Hannan, argued at the final conference of the U.S. Bishops' Peace Pastoral that the theory must allow a city population to be killed if weapons are kept in that city. Otherwise, the war will be lost. Any limitations the theory places on a country at war makes it less likely for that country to win the war. So in this way advocates of the theory stretch the theory to allow killing without limit. For example, during the Vietnam War, if it had been decided not to bomb the dykes to flood the rice fields, gun emplacements would have been put on the dykes. Obviously, it was argued, it is permissible to bomb the dykes and starve the people

anyway. This example shows how even the basic claim of the theory—that it is a theory of limiting war—is shown to be false. It is twisted into a theory that allows war under the pretense of limiting it.

13. The writings and work of persons like Fuchs, McCormick, Schillibeeckx, and others, demonstrate that moral theology is historically conditioned and historically constituted. It is made up of concrete judgments made in the light of historical reality. All this is missing in the Just-Unjust War Theory as it is proposed.

When we look at the Just-Unjust War Theory in its historical context, we find that acceptance of the theory as a moral guide has led Western civilization along a path of horror: the examples are wars of religion that set Christian against Christian, Christian against heretics, and the Christians against Muslims during the Crusades—and all this blessed by the popes.

In World War II, the Just-Unjust War Theory was preached by churches on both sides. Cardinal Mercier of France preached to parents, wives, and children of French soldiers that their loved ones were not only heroes, but martyrs for the faith. German Catholic bishops called on their people to support Hitler's war for folk and homeland.[19] All of these evils throw historical light on what the Just War Theory is by showing what it does.

14. The theory is essentially a theory of limiting war. There is abundant evidence that once nuclear war starts, it cannot be controlled or limited.

Any of these weaknesses would be serious. Taken together, they show that the theory is at least outdated, and probably never has been valid. Yet it is the only attempt at a moral justification of war by Christians. If rejected, the Christian is left with the gospel, which rejects killing as immoral. Why? Because the theory is proposed as an "exception" to the gospel of love. It does not deny that we are obliged to universal love. It states that the fulfillment of set conditions creates an "exception," i.e., a set of conditions so exceptional that when they are all fulfilled, the gospel law of love is not violated, but fulfilled. Once one is convinced that these circumstances are so exceptional that they can never exist, all that remains for the Christian is the law of love.

Benefit of Doubt

If you can't agree in your own mind that all of the conditions required for the war are fulfilled with regard to a particular war, a Christian may be left in doubt as to how to act. What then? Most people accept the word of their government. "The government has the facts. The government knows more than you do." This was the retort I got during the Vietnam War when I tried to show that the Vietnam War did not fulfill the conditions of the theory.

My answer to this is that it was not enough for the government to know more. The government has to give the facts to me so fully that I can judge without doubt that the war fulfills all of the conditions of the Just-Unjust War Theory. Otherwise, according to the theory I cannot go to war. In the matter of my taking life, hidden reasons are not enough; probability that the government has good reasons is not enough. The taking of human life is forbidden. It is not a neutral matter. It is forbidden. On other matters, authority may have the benefit of doubt, but not where the taking of life is concerned. There, it must prove its case lucidly and fully before a believer in the Just-Unjust War Theory can accept any orders to kill.

If there is any doubt, the practitioner of the Just-Unjust War Theory must refuse. Governments derive their authority from God. They never have authority to violate God's laws, nor may I give government the benefit of doubt when it orders me to violate divine law.

The Just-Unjust War Theory is essentially an effort to remove from war those characteristics that make it morally repulsive, for example, murder, greed, desire for power, deceit, hatred. But when that is done, you no longer have war. That is why the Just-Unjust War tradition is not, and never was, seriously followed by any nation. No nation accepts it as policy today, or ever did.

Jim Finn, author of *Politics, Protest and Peace,* and one of the most able exponents of the Just-Unjust War tradition, ended an explanation of the theory with the story of Eisenhower getting into an elevator at the Pentagon and saying, "Take me to the eighth floor."

"I am sorry, sir. There is no eighth floor. We don't go that high."

Eisenhower smiled and replied. "All right. Just take me as far as you can."

Finn concluded, "The Just-Unjust War Theory is like that elevator. It does not get you to peace. It is an unsuccessful effort to make rational something which is essentially irrational, war. But it is good as far as it goes."

I disagree with that. It does more harm than good. It is used as a front for accepting all wars. Even when it is not used, it gives Christians the impression that they have some Christian basis for accepting war. It not only doesn't get you to peace, it does get you to war. If the goal is peace, then peaceful means should be used to attain that goal. The theory is a two-edged sword. It has both a "restraining" and "justification" or "apologetic" function. This second function predominates and outweighs the first. The bad outweighs the good.

Many Catholic moralists, influenced by Pope John XXIII, Vatican II, and the destructive capability of nuclear technology, have rejected the Just-Unjust War Theory. Pope John XXIII saw any war as a denial of the unity of the human family. In his great encyclical *Peace on Earth*, he said, "There can be no doubt that relations between states, as between individuals, should be regulated not by the force of arms, but by the light of reason; by rule that is of truth, of justice, and one of active and sincere cooperation" (par. 114).

Pope John XXIII had confidence in the human spirit's permanent capacity to open itself to truth. He saw the failure of Christians to trust in the truth of faith, and their willingness to resort to the use of force as a failure of faith. He declared that peace is to be found not in "equality of arms, but in mutual trust alone."

Pope John's theology called not for nuclear deterrence, but for a worldwide community. The Council Fathers were unable entirely to share John's vision, but his vision was put before them, and they responded in some measure.

In the *Constitution on the Church in the Modern World* (par. 80), Vatican II presented a new perspective on war. At the beginning of the statement, it calls for "an evaluation of war with an entirely new attitude" because of the almost total slaughter which threatens humankind from the new weapons.

Article 77 sets the frame of reference for the discussion with the subtitle "The Human Family's Hour of Crisis." Chapter V, Part II, carries the title "The Fostering of Peace and the Promoting of a Community of Nations."

These two elements, the solidarity of the human family and the thermonuclear danger, make up the context for the entire discussion of war.

The council summarizes the attitude with these three elements: a condemnation of area destruction; an appeal to conscience that calls on those in the armed services not to obey authority blindly, but to weigh the morality of the orders they follow; and the advocacy of nonviolence as a specific way of following the gospel.

With regard to area destruction, the council said: "Any act of war, aimed indiscriminately at the destruction of entire cities or extensive areas along with their population, is a crime against God and man himself. It merits unequivocal and unhesitating condemnation" (par. 80). In its entire text, this is the only time that the word "condemnation" is used. Because of the use of this word and the importance of the statement, this passage in a sense became the central declaration of the entire council.

With this statement the council moved the Catholic Church away from the acceptance of the Just-Unjust War Theory. There is no reference here to the weighing of conditions. What this statement says is that the moral limits of war are bypassed when thermonuclear destruction or area destruction is in question. The shift from the Just-Unjust War framework, back to the gospel of peace of the first three Christian centuries, has become a fact. Discussion of this statement in the council proceedings by Bishop Taylor of Sweden makes the new position most emphatic. Bishop Taylor offered the following statement as an amendment:

As total war is now a war against God's plan, against mankind itself, the actuation of the spirit of Christ is more

imperative than ever. Christians should cultivate a deep
awareness that violence is an actual expression of hatred,
and should undertake a fuller exploration of the non-violent love, the teaching of Christ. [20]

The second element that the council introduced in the
new vision on war is conscience. The council praised
conscience with these words: "Actions which deliberately
conflict with these same principles (natural law), as well
as orders commanding such actions, are criminal, and
blind obedience cannot excuse those who yield to them"
(par. 79). This is in keeping with the Nuremberg tribunal
which said that officers who followed orders are responsible for their actions. They cannot shift their responsibility
for immoral actions to those who ordered the actions. The
United States accepted this idea in the treaty at London.

The final element in the new perspective on peace offered by the council is a return to nonviolence. The
council said, "We cannot fail to praise those who
renounce the use of violence in the vindication of their
rights, and who resort to methods of defense which are
otherwise available to the weaker parties, too" (sec. 78).

These three elements of a new perspective on peace are
not part of a Just-Unjust War Theory. They clearly and
positively point out the path toward peace. It is not a
precise and specific path, but it does indicate the way.
The new way initiates a return to the gospel of love and
peace. The gospel depicts Christ as a lamb and not as a
wolf, and the Spirit of God as a dove and not an eagle. It
brings back the gospel story which speaks of Christ as a
Prince of Peace, not a soldier at arms.

This is the spirit reflected by Vatican II. Instead of trying to show that, under certain conditions, some wars

might be just, it makes clear that certain acts of war are wrong. It points out the Christian mission of peace, and emphasizes that the Christian gospel is opposed to all war.

Other Christian leaders reflect this trend away from all war. Karl Barth, the heroic Protestant pastor, who coauthored the "Barman Resolution" confronting Hitler's domination of the churches during World War II, asked (in 1959) that the mainline Christian churches confront their governments on the immorality of nuclear war, as the most urgent moral issue of our times. John Howard Yoder, John Ferguson, Ronald Sider, Richard Taylor, Jean Lasserre, Millard C. Lind, G. H. C. Macgregor, James Douglass, Edgar W. Orr, Gordon Zahn, and A. Trocmé are writers of today who call Christians to follow the gospel of peace.

In an address at a meeting of the Dutch military chaplaincy, Cardinal Alfrink, primate of the Netherlands, took the position that a just war is no longer possible, holding that the existence of nuclear weapons excludes the existence of a just war, because the means that could be used to fight injustice, would cause much greater injustices.[21]

Cardinal Lercaro of Bologna dismissed the idea of just war as something "left over from the cases and mental attitudes which no longer have anything to do with the facts."

The same idea is expressed by Bishop Giuseppe Marafini, president of the Italian Bishops' Ecumenical Secretariat. At the August 1969 meeting, he declared, "For the church, any war is an inhuman, anti-evangelical and an inadequate means for solving differences"[22] He said the teaching of Pope John XXIII, Vatican II, and

Pope Paul VI illustrates the change in the church's attitude toward war. It is a movement away from the acceptance of any war, toward a rediscovery of the gospel message of peace. It is clear that the council brought down the curtain on the Just-Unjust War Theory.

The theory was much talked about by theologians, but it had never received any formal theoretical approval from any council of the church. At Vatican Council II, some bishops tried to have the Just-Unjust War Theory acknowledged and accepted. This was never done. No formal reference to the theory was ever made, not even in a footnote. (The claim that Vatican II allowed for a war in self-defense is denied for reasons explained in chapter six of this book.)

The Just Adultery Theory

To illustrate how inadequate the Just-Unjust War Theory is, consider an analogy, the Just Adultery Theory. A look at it helps us see how differently Christians respond to murder and adultery. A Christian minister or priest who openly preaches the Just Adultery Theory would be run out of his church; not so with the Just-Unjust War Theory. Yet both theories violate equally commandments of God: "Thou shall not kill," and "Thou shall not commit adultery." Both set up conditions to get around the commandments. Conditions for just adultery are:

1. Last resort

Every other means of getting along must be first tried: discussion, advice of a third party, reconciliation of differences, expressions of affection, anything short of adultery.

2. Good intention

There must be no intent to harm one's spouse or any other person. Revenge for unfaithfulness of one's partner would not be considered a sufficient cause, nor would the need for more children, or a second home. The cause must be a genuine love and affection for the companion in adultery that cannot be satisfied in any other way and, conversely, a genuine need of that love and affection on the part of the one initiating the adultery. The main point to be kept in mind is that the adultery must be in defense of love. There must be a pure intention. This condition entirely excludes aggressive adultery, which is sometimes called "rape."

Parallel to the altruistic intention required in the Just War Theory, the motive must be to save the life or lives of others. This could be done by contributing to the war effort (even in peacetime) by using adultery in the "diplomatic" corps to gain crucial information for national defense. Both men and women could be registered and conscripted for adulterous service if there were not enough volunteers. Parallel to ROTC (Reserve Officers Training Corps) there might be established a ROAC (Reserve Officers Adultery Corps).

3. Protection of the innocent

The aggrieved partner must not be harmed. Every effort at secrecy must be made; no open flaunting or even informing the aggrieved partner would be consistent with this condition. If children are born of the adultery, both partners to the act must have the intention of caring for the children. The use of a contraceptive device, or the intent of having an abortion, violate this condition and make the adultery immoral.

7286/

4. Proportionality.

A favorable balance of good over evil must be reasonably hoped for. The foreseeable harm to absent partners and to living children must be weighed against the need of affection and love on the part of the adulterers. This need must honestly predominate over the cumulative harm.

The damage to family life, and the weakening of respect for the marriage bond, must be offset by the marked increase in human love, affection, and respect for the human person that is endangered by the social effects of adultery.

Provided these conditions are all fulfilled, adultery is not a violation of the gospel but an act of love and mercy. Absurd?

Perhaps, but less absurd than the Just-Unjust War Theory. Adultery is a personal act. It does not kill millions of people, or even one person. It does not have government support. It always allows for the possibility of repentance and reconciliation that is precluded by killing. On balance, the Just Adultery Theory has much more in its favor, than the Just-Unjust War Theory. Why is it, then, that most Christians understand the weaknesses of the Just Adultery Theory, but are blind to the greater weaknesses of the Just-Unjust War Theory? Could it be that we consider morality to be limited to individuals and to personal conduct, and that what a group or a government does is beyond the limits of morality?

Or do we put the authority of the government above that of God? If a president, king, dictator, or general says an action is necessary for the defense of a country, do we say a Christian may do it and not be guilty of sin? Since the president knows more about what is required for national security than anyone else, then each Christian can obey in good conscience. It follows that if the leader says, "Rape," the Christian rapes. If the leader says "Kill," the Christian kills.

If as a follower of Jesus a person can intentionally kill another human because a president says it is okay, then surely he can rape another if a president, king, or dictator orders it.

Can we serve both God and government when the government orders what God forbids?

CHAPTER SIX

Answers to Objections to Pacifism

Some of the strongest arguments against Christian pacifism come from Reinhold Niebuhr, who was a pacifist before Hitler came to power. His books, *Why the Christian Church Is Not Pacifist* and *Moral Man and Immoral Society* made him the most influential Protestant theologian opposed to pacifism. He writes with the understanding developed in his years of pacifism.

Niebuhr prefaces his arguments with important concessions to pacifism. He agrees that Jesus was a pacifist. "It is very foolish to deny that the ethic of Jesus is an absolute and uncompromising ethic. . . . The injunctions 'resist not evil,' 'love your enemies,' 'be not anxious for your life' are all of one piece, and they are all uncompromising and absolute."[23] Niebuhr supports the pacifist position when he says that when Christians take up arms there is nothing in either the teaching or example of Jesus that would justify them in saying they are imitating Jesus. "Nothing is more futile and pathetic than the effort of some Christian theologians, who find it necessary to become involved in the relativities of politics . . . to justify themselves by seeking to prove that Christ was also involved in some of these relativities; that He used whips to drive the money changers out of the Temple, or that He

came 'not to bring peace but the sword.' "[24] He says that
the debate between the pacifist and the nonpacifist is not
about Jesus' pacifism, but only about the extent Jesus
intended it to be used in an imperfect world. The question is not "Does Jesus command this?" (Does Jesus require pacifism?) Rather, the question is: "Does he mean
us to obey what appears to be a plain command?"

Argument 1. The Lesser Evil

Niebuhr argues that the gospel cannot be applied
directly to politics and cannot be lived out. It was written
for a rural community two thousand years ago, not for the
present industrial state. It cannot be applied directly. National states cannot live according to the Beatitudes.
However, the gospel can be a norm to discriminate
between the lesser of two evils—a guide to show us how
far off we are from the ideal. This is the function of the
gospel. It is not a direct guide for us in deciding for or
against war. The strength of this argument is that the
gospel is used; it is not put aside, but it is used as a "discriminate norm."

What does "discriminate norm" mean? It means that
the gospel helps us decide, among the alternatives open
to us, which one is more in accord with the ideal of
unconditional love taught in the gospel. For example, it
could have been (and was) argued during the Vietnam
War that it is more in accord with the ideal of universal
love that the U.S. go to war with North Vietnam, rather
than do nothing and let communism overwhelm South
Vietnam and cause its people to suffer. In this way the
gospel has become a discriminate norm. Supposedly, the
lesser of two evils has been chosen.

I give extra attention to this argument about the "lesser

evil" because it is often used, and it is often encountered in confrontations with nonpacifists. To begin with, a clarification is needed between physical evils like sickness or surgery and moral evils like murder.

All of us face situations where alternative choices include two evils: for example, we may suffer in accepting surgery or suffer without it. Mostly, they are choices of physical evil or suffering. This is not the same as "choosing the lesser evil" in Niebuhr's sense. He is talking about choosing between a moral evil, such as killing the tyrant, and a physical evil, such as accepting his tyranny. When I choose a moral evil in order to accomplish some good, I am acting far differently than when I am choosing between two physical evils.

First Reply to "The Lesser Evil"

God never requires us to sin. To believe that God ever puts us in a situation where we are compelled to commit sin by deliberate choice makes nonsense of the gospel message that God's grace is sufficient for us, that God will help us in every need, in every temptation, to do what is right, not what is evil. "You can trust God not to let you be tried beyond your strength, and with any trial he will give you a way out of it and the strength to bear it" (1 Cor. 10:13, JB).

If God required us to sin, then God would be the cause of sin. This is blasphemy. It makes God the source of evil. God does not require us to do moral evil (sin) in order that good may come of it. God does not ask us to use a moral evil means to achieve a good goal.

Second Reply to "The Lesser Evil"

Between the two ways of sinning, that is, accepting

either war or tyranny, there is always a third alternative: nonviolent resistance. It may be very difficult, yet it is the way of the cross exemplified by Jesus. In fact, Jesus was faced with the dilemma of the "lesser evil." In his cause, the founding of the kingdom, he was endangered by enemies.

If he were killed, his disciples would be scattered and leaderless. If he wished he could have asked his Father who would have promptly sent more than twelve legions of angels to his defense (Mt. 26:53).

He could have put aside his unconditional love ethic. He did not. He believed that sacrificial love could completely change a situation and create most unexpected consequences. He chose the cross, and the result was not defeat but resurrection and victory over death and suffering.

Third Reply to "The Lesser Evil"

Is war ever the lesser evil? Once the passions of war and nationalism are aroused, is it ever possible to make a relatively unbiased judgment which is clear and compelling enough to justify action—an action which would otherwise be condemned by the same ethic on which we base our "lesser evil" objection?

Consider the Vietnam War. We know now from the Pentagon Papers that we were lied to about the facts of the war, about the casualties of the war. We know from Senate testimony that we were lied to about the facts that led to the Tonkin Gulf Resolution on which the first actions of the war were based. Was it possible for anyone to look ahead and see what this war would cost us, and on the basis of that decision decide that it was clearly the lesser of two evils?

Consider World War II. Could the ordinary person or anyone else foresee how the alliance to defeat Hitler would make the Soviets and the U.S. world powers, poised at each other's throats, ready to destroy themselves and the world with nuclear weapons? If they could foresee it and all the other evil consequences, could they judge it to be clearly the lesser of two evils?

The burden of proof is on the government or individual who chooses war. The making of war is a great evil. It is not clear what good comes of it. It demands loyalty to a national state in place of loyalty to the way of universal love that forbids war. War brings with it many evils: murder, rape, starvation, lying, hunger, nakedness, plague, cruelty, hatred, loss of faith, despair, and all the other related evils.

When all the consequences of war are balanced against the consequences of not killing, war surely begins to appear the worse evil, not the lesser. Only when we blind ourselves to the moral evils that are an essential part of war, only when we consider killing to be morally good, can we find war a lesser evil.

Fourth Reply to "The Lesser Evil"

The first question a Christian should ask should not be "Which is the lesser evil?" but, "What does God want me to do? What would Christ have done? Is war Christ's way?" If the answer is that Christ's way is not war, but the cross, then by choosing that way we invite God's help that can transform us and change the situation. The cross, the way of nonviolent revolution, is always an alternative beyond war and surrender, for both individuals and nations. The Christian never needs to choose only among evils.

Fifth Reply to "the Lesser Evil"

A weakness of the argument for the "lesser evil" can be illustrated by an example. Suppose I consider the bombing of a nuclear power plant under construction a lesser evil than allowing it to operate. Would it be morally right for me to bomb the plant to destroy it? All governments would say, "No." Yet these same governments use the "lesser evil" argument in their own favor when they make war. This limiting of the application to circumstances favoring oneself exposes the double-standard underlying its use.

Argument 2. People Are Sinful

People are so sinful, the argument goes, that they are incapable of the unselfish love ethic of Jesus. There is a gulf between a perfect God and sinful humans, a gulf so great that no love ethic can bridge it. War is justified because people are sinners and must be coerced. International order is always dependent upon balance of power. This condition is due to human sinfulness.

Reply to "People Are Sinful"

This argument springs from an unscriptural view of human nature. On purely rational grounds (assuming that humans are naturally aggressive), the argument would do better.

Do the gospels present humans as sinners who must be driven by force? The gospels give a different picture. Jesus saw the world as God's world, not "wholly other" than God's world. He drew his lessons from birds and flowers, from the growth and work of people. He saw God in persons like John the Baptist. He saw good in an ex-sinner, Mary Magdalene. When a sinner comes "to himself," the sinner arises and goes to his father (the prodigal son). The mustard seed grows secretly—the nature of the world fosters the growth of God's purposes. Nature is on God's side. He taught us to pray, "Thy will be done on earth."

Paul's epistles corroborate this gospel view of human nature. Because creation is redeemed, continuance in sin is intolerable. There is a loving personal relationship between God and his creation. This excludes a theology like Niebuhr's that separates the natural from the redeemed and regards nature as depraved.

Niebuhr's pessimistic view of human nature contradicts the joy and hope of the gospel. It sees the incarnation as a divine intrusion, instead of the appearance of a brother.

In this view of human depravity there is no room for the indwelling of the Holy Spirit, and for "enabling" grace. God dwells in us and we call God "our Father." Niebuhr sees grace as "pardon" rather than "power." Yet grace is "power." It is an essential part of Paul's faith.

Paul speaks of being "helped only by his power driving me irresistibly." Paul boasts, "There is nothing I cannot master with the help of One who gives me strength" (Phil. 4:13, JB). According to Paul, the servant of Christ is capable of perfect obedience because he or she is transformed in the make up of his or her being as a child of God.

Argument 3. Personal, Not Group Morality

Morality is concerned with my personal relationships. I do not rob, rape, or murder my neighbor. Morality does not apply in the same way to war. The state is not bound by personal morality. It is amoral and follows military necessity. It may be guided by some type of ethics, but not by morality. Morality is personal.

Reply to "Personal, Not Group Morality"

This is Niebuhr's argument on "moral man and immoral society." It assumes the separation of private and public morality. This is false when applied to the state. As Pope John XXIII writes in his letter *Peace on Earth:* "The same rights and obligations that apply to the individual apply to groups." It is even more false when applied to the church. The church is a group. Should the church be considered an amoral group?

The church, with divine help, has the mission of making known the truth and leading people to the truth. Its example is meant to help individual morality. According to God's plan the church can lead the way to divine truth. It is not meant to be less moral than the individual. It can lead and help the individual. This is one group—the very one Niebuhr talks about—that disproves his argument. The same is true of all other groups. They are made up of humans—all subject to God's laws. Whatever the group does as a group—a state or an army—is either in accord with morality or opposed to morality.

Argument 4. Self-Defense

What about self-defense? Doesn't a nation have a right to defend itself?

First Reply to "Self-Defense"[25]

Self-defense is not a gospel principle. It is a principle of reason used by Cicero and Aristotle long before Christ's time. Christ did not defend himself when the soldiers came to arrest him. He taught that redemption comes from accepting suffering, not from inflicting suffering on others. Whoever would save his life must lose it.

Second Reply to "Self-Defense"

Self-defense by immoral means is contrary to the gospel. For example, when a medical doctor wants to help a woman who has an unwanted pregnancy, he may not kill the child to relieve the woman. Neither may a government kill because it wants to defend its people. A good end does not justify the use of an evil means.

Third Reply to "Self-Defense"

There is no known or foreseeable defense against nuclear missiles. Even a fully working anti-ballistic missile system (and no one has such a system) would at *best* stop only one missile out of five. Weapons have evolved to the point where national states can no longer defend themselves. Just as the development of long-range cannons ended the era of the city-states with their fortified walls, so the era of ballistic nuclear weapons ends the era of the nation state. We are already in an international world—a world of transnational corporations, worldwide communication, and transportation. Preparing nuclear weapons today may provide deterrence or offense, but not defense.

Even deterrence gives no security when you consider the spread of nuclear weapons. Experts predict that within a few years at least 20 nations will have nuclear weapons. The deterrence program of today is leading to war, not peace. History is full of weapons buildups that were meant to deter but resulted instead in their use. This is even more certain in the nuclear age.

A book by the British General Stephen King-Hall, *Defense in a Nuclear Age*, argues that the military betrays

England if they plan any strategy that includes nuclear weapons. Any nuclear exchange would reduce England to a radioactive ash heap. On a straight military strategy basis, he argues how the British should, step-by-step, renounce use of nuclear weapons; form a political alliance with nonnuclear powers; step up the war of ideas—psychological, political, and economic; reduce conventional forces to a token border control group; and begin to think of war as resistance to occupation after it occurs.

At the same time the people might begin to think about how to stand up for, or die for, what they really believe in, under occupation. General King-Hall sees the risk that this might not work—that all would be killed—but he also sees some possibility that it might succeed. He sees no possibility at all in the use of nuclear weapons succeeding. To him, military experts who recommend a nuclear strategy for England are guilty of treason. The question presupposes that there is some method of defense in the nuclear age.

One way to answer it is to retort, "How would you do it?" Obviously, it can't be done. Even with space technology, the majority of missiles would simply pass each other in the air, or so close to the ground, that they would escape detection by radar.

Fourth Reply to "Self-Defense"

Self-defense may be the argument of a tyrant or of a state that deserves punishment, rather than continued existence. God asked Isaiah and Jeremiah to warn the chosen people not to defend themselves against threatening enemies, since God was using these enemies to punish Israel for her sins. Does God want a defense of each and every state?

Fifth Reply to "Self-Defense"

Self-defense is falsely used to cover all sorts of aggression. What is self-defense or "living space" for Hitler is aggression in the eyes of many others. South Africa today argues its right to self-defense, but what it defends is the right of a minority government of whites to exclude blacks from a decent life in their own homeland. The United States could not honestly argue self-defense in its wars against the American Indians. The United States used the "domino" theory to argue that our war in Vietnam was self-defense.

The word "self-defense" has many broad meanings. If it is to have any validity at all, it must be clearly defined. A usable definition might be a defense which uses moral means (not killing) against an unjust aggression. "Moral means" might be the strategy of nonviolent action such as that organized by Gandhi in the defense of India against British domination or by Martin Luther King, Jr., against racism in the U.S. "Self-defense" of this kind is more in line with the gospel.

Sixth Reply to "Self-Defense"

Mary, the mother of Jesus, stood by her Son's cross as he was crucified. She did not try to organize some defense for her Son whom she knew to be innocent. She accepted her Son's teaching, that suffering and death are redemptive. "Unless the grain of wheat falls into the ground, it will not bear fruit." "He that would save his life must lose it." "I must suffer and be put to death by evil men and on the third day, rise again."

Argument 5. Protecting Your Loved Ones

A question like this is often put to pacifists: "If you

were walking down the street with your mother and she was attacked by a robber who intended to rob and rape her, would you just stand by and do nothing, or would you defend her?"

If you would defend her, even by killing the robber if necessary, then you should also accept a use of defense of the innocent.

First Reply to "Protecting Your Loved Ones"

This is not war, but a person-to-person conflict. I cannot justify the use of weapons of mass destruction to kill all the relatives and innocent fellow citizens of the robber in order to stop his attack on a loved one. Even if I killed the robber (and I don't agree that such killing is moral), the parallel to war is false. War means killing people. In a person-to-person conflict I don't rely on the word of a government. In this case I see and know what is going on without any intermediary.

Second Reply to "Protecting Your Loved Ones"

Even St. Augustine, who first formulated the Just-Unjust War Theory, says that I may never kill on private authority even to save life.

Third Reply to "Protecting Your Loved Ones"

Killing the robber is never the only means I have of defending a loved one. I could do something else short of killing. I could put my body between the robber and my loved one, scream for help, try ways of physically thwarting the robber, or even simply give him the money if that's what he's after.[26]

What I do will depend a great deal on the attitude I have before the robber appears. If I believe that, as a last resort, I must be ready to kill robbers, then I will carry a gun. If I do carry a gun, my gun may be the reason the robber uses his gun. (In Britain, where the police do not use guns, there is much less killing of police and criminals than in the U.S.) If I do not believe in killing, even as a last resort, then I will not have a gun when the robber appears.

In summary, I would not kill. I cannot imagine circumstances where the only alternative I have is killing. The intent to kill the criminal may endanger my loved one as well. Neither do I consider taking a human life on a par with losing money or enduring rape, though these are also terrible human acts.

Fourth Reply to "Protecting Your Loved Ones"

This question poses a hypothetical situation which is used to justify real-life mass murder. My mother is long dead (God be good to her), yet every day the military of the world prepares young men and women to kill and orders them to kill. This horrible situation is not justified by an appeal to my love for my long dead mother.

This is like one of the hypothetical questions used by abortionists: "Would you like to help curb the levels of misery, poverty, and child abuse that families in our country suffer?" The answer from anyone with a social conscience is always "of course I would," but this doesn't justify abortion as a means of alleviating misery. An advocate of abortion, though, can take this good question and turn it into a hypothetical justification for innumerable abortions in the same way that the military takes good questions, such as, "What is our level of love for our family?" and twists them to justify its countless crimes.

On the hypothesis that I would defend my mother's

life, I am asked to go along with nuclear warfare that would kill hundreds of millions of people in any major exchange between nuclear powers. If my mother were alive, she would most likely be killed also. I would not be defending her; it's all a lie. The military's hypothetical question of protecting my mother has two answers—one purely hypothetical and the other based in reality. The hypothetical answer, that of the military, is that my mother will be protected by them. The other answer, based in reality, is that she will not be.

I am certain though that if my mother were alive today, she would not want to be "protected" at the expense of millions of other mothers, their husbands, children, friends, and homes. In her life she seemed to always put greater emphasis on the real than on the hypothetical.

Fifth Reply to "Protecting Your Loved Ones"

A robber who is intent on killing would not be ready to enter into the presence of God. As a Christian I would be more ready to meet God if I gave my life for my loved one and spared the robber so he might have time to repent before death.

Argument 6. What About the Russians?

What about the Russians? It would be very nice if we could put aside our arms because of belief in the gospel, but the Russians don't believe in the gospel. If we lay down our arms, the Russians will walk all over us, so we need to keep the upper hand militarily (or at least maintain an equal pace in the arms race).

First Reply to "What About the Russians"

Americans like to imagine that U.S. military policy is

more moral than the Soviet Union's because we tend to categorize ourselves as a "Christian" country, possessing some sort of morals, and the USSR as an atheist one. But is there really much difference? Are we a "light to the world," pressing peace or are we an aggressive participant pushing militaristic competition to even higher and more dangerous levels.

We are invited directly by God to follow the gospel. Our response is not conditioned by what the Russians do. We are not asked to go just as far as others go. We are asked to follow God—to take up our cross, to be lights to the world—whether others do it or not. Jesus did not say, "Love others if they love you." His commands are not reciprocal, dependent on the response of others.

Second Reply to "What About the Russians"

The Russians have been second in every initiative of the nuclear age. The U.S. first developed the atom bomb. We used it first on Hiroshima and Nagasaki. We first developed the H-bomb, submarine missiles, MIRV (multiple-targeted, independent re-entry vehicles), the ABM (anti-ballistic missiles), the cruise missiles, the Trident submarine with long-range maneuverability, mirved missiles, and the neutron bomb.

We have demonstrated a "win" mentality. Never have we been content with preparing for defense or deterrence. For this reason, in the early days when we alone had the bomb we refused to put it under some kind of international control or to renounce further development of it. Many of our experts, agree with Secretary Robert McNamara that we need no more than two hundred to four hundred megatons—delivered on target, to deter any of our enemies. Yet we have gone on making more and more nuclear weapons until we have over thirty-five thousand nuclear war-heads in our arsenal, and are currently spending billions of dollars for research and development of more and newer nuclear weapons. This is evidence of our seeking to "win" instead of "defend." We cannot honestly blame the Russians for all this.

The development of weaponry with potential for greater and greater accuracy, like the cruise and Trident missiles, are also evidence of our strategy to "win." These weapons are capable of very accurately hitting the Russian missile silos. These silos would presumably be empty in a war of defense. Less accurate bombs would suffice if we were merely thinking of defense or even retaliation.

What about the Russians? They are always hastening to follow what we do. They, too, are burdened, politically and economically, by the arms race. Their survival, like ours, is at stake. Maybe they would respond to a 10 percent reduction of the arms race. The risk in trying this is nothing compared to the risk of continuing the race.

We do have a good example of a peaceful initiative by the U.S. that was responded to in kind by the USSR. In 1963, President Kennedy ordered a halt to U.S. nuclear testing in the atmosphere without requiring a signed agreement before he took this important step. The presidentially ordered nuclear testing halt was to continue so long as the Soviets and other countries did not test. The Soviets responded favorably and a Soviet-American deadlock was broken. The result was the signing of the Limited Test Ban Treaty by the U.S. and the USSR. This treaty has been the most important achievement in the long history of arms control negotiations between the U.S. and the USSR.

With regard to our belief in the gospel, how does our belief show itself as different from the Russians when we ring them with bases, and continue to develop more and more weapons? We threaten to kill them massively. How can they see any light of the gospel in our plans or actions? How are we any better than the Russians in our attitude toward war and the taking of human lives? If we were Russians, would we see the U.S. as gospel-oriented, and gospel-directed? We publicly assert our separation of church and state. Does the church have any separate military policy from the state? The answer should be "yes." The church is opposed to the use of nuclear weapons for any reason.

Argument 7. Pacifism Is Not Practical

Pacifism is not practical. It does not work in the real world. It is a naive solution to a complex problem. This is one of the most prominent generalizations used against the gospel of peace.

Reply to "Pacifism Is Not Practical"

Nothing is more impractical than making more nuclear weapons and hoping for peace through them. Whether pacifism is practical or not depends on what you think of the cross of Christ. Obviously, Christ thought it was the way to establish his Kingdom and to bring peace on earth. In this sense he considered it practical. But in order to work it has to be practiced. There is no evidence that it does not work where it is tried.

There is abundant evidence that wars do not bring peace. Instead, they set the conditions for the next war. In the nuclear age, our technology is proof to persons without faith that nuclear weapons will not bring peace.

Is it practical to try for peace without any reference to God? The gospel tells us that the way to peace is through the paradox of the cross; the program for peace is detailed in the Beatitudes. In the sense that peace is God's work and humans are God's instruments, peace is never just the result of human effort, and never practical in the sense of being done by human power alone.

Argument 8. What Alternative Is There?

If you oppose war, you must offer some alternative. What is your alternative to war?

First Reply to "What Alternative Is There?"

An alternative is another way of achieving the same result. War is so evil with such evil results, that no substitute way of achieving the same evils is likely to be found. The presupposition of this argument is that war brings peace or protects peace. The Christian belief is that God and humans, working together according to the pattern set out in the gospel, bring peace. War is not part of this program. War brings more war. The reason why Christians have had such little peace and have such small hopes for peace is that they have deserted the gospel in the seeking of peace and sought it through war.

It is not inherently obligatory to pose an alternative to war when pointing out war's evils. The mere pointing out of the evil is a good work in itself. So if I point out that lying, robbery, rape, and oppression of the poor are evils, I do something good. Perhaps I will be listened to more closely if I suggest some alternative. Something better can be suggested, even though it is not an alternative in the sense that it achieves the same results as the evil.

As an alternative to war, I suggest imitating Christ,

following the pattern of gospel living according to the Beatitudes, and organizing that pattern along the lines followed by Gandhi in India and by Martin Luther King, Jr., in the U.S. If only a small part of the time, talent, and treasure spent on preparing for and supporting war were put into training for nonviolent actions for peace, much good could be accomplished.

On the individual level I think we should begin with refusing to pay taxes for nuclear weapons and for other war preparations. It is a contradiction to pay for war while we pray for peace. If Christians on the basis of conscience organized resistance to war taxes, there would be changes in our national policy of military spending and preparing for war. The trust that we thus put in following God speaking to us through conscience would become our alternative—our "better way" than war.

Second Reply to "What Alternative Is There?"

This question presupposes what isn't true. It presupposes that at the present time our arms give us security. It presupposes that the more arms we have, the more security we will have. Neither of these statements are true in the nuclear age. We have no security now.

We cannot defend ourselves, and so as an alternative to our present insecurity—our inability to defend ourselves from the nuclear weapons of our enemies—there are various possibilities. One is presented in the book by General Stephen A. King-Hall, *The Defense of the Nuclear Age*, in which he, from a professional military strategy point of view, shows that the use of nuclear weapons will result in reducing Great Britain to a radioactive ash heap. So the realistic military strategy should begin with overcoming the mental block which says that we can only overcome force with more force, and with studying nonviolent ways of organizing against an invasion once the invasion has taken place. In his book King-Hall shows how there is some hope his strategy will succeed, but no hope at all in going on with the arms race. And that is true of the U.S. also.

There is no hope militarily of the arms race bringing peace or security to the U.S. The more the U.S. advances its nuclear technology and nuclear stockpiling, the less hope for peace there is. So from a strictly technological point of view, from the strength of our weapons and the direction in which we are going, three alternatives are possible: some sort of a national organizing toward nonviolence, trying to bring the rest of the world in line as King-Hall suggests; some sort of federation of the nations of the world to work as the world federalists do; a world government with a federation of supporting states with the prohibition of national armies that would interfere with it.

Argument 9. Unilateral Disarmament

Unilateral nuclear disarmament is insane. For instance, if you are out on the desert and a wild tribesman is bearing down on you, do you go out and kneel down and ask for mercy? He would run you right through with his sword. The least you can do, if you have to die, is to die fighting (and killing), taking as many of the enemy with you as you can. The same is true of nuclear weapons.

First Reply to "Unilateral Disarmament"

The first question that a Christian should ask about unilateral disarmament is, "What are the circumstances, and what should a Christian do in those circumstances?"

The circumstances of nuclear deterrence are that both sides are fully able and ready to destroy each other, no matter who starts the war. This is not the case of the wild desert swordsman—so the analogy does not apply.

Second Reply to "Unilateral Disarmament"

Why was the tribesman attacking? If you had weapons and were coming to his home and had previously threatened to destroy him, the attack might be due to your conduct. In that case, you would be the aggressor. But if you changed your mind, put aside your weapons, went out and asked "mercy," there would be some possibility that your change would change him. Even if it did not, your death in such a case would be far more an imitation of Christ than going ahead with your aggression.

Third Reply to "Unilateral Disarmament"

If the case is that of two armed tribesmen, both constantly threatening to kill each other, and it ends in a confrontation in which both are killed, neither have acted as a Christian should—with love for each other because of faith in God. Both die uselessly and in defiance of God's law. This case makes clear the relationship between our faith, our thought processes, and our action. If we have faith in God and live according to it, our actions are different than they would be without that faith.

Fourth Reply to "Unilateral Disarmament"

Even from a military point of view, unilateral nuclear disarmament makes more sense than going on with the arms race. (See the viewpoint presented by British General Stephen King-Hall, in *Defense in The Nuclear Age,* which was discussed earlier in this chapter.)

Fifth Reply to "Unilateral Disarmament"

Nuclear weapons have become a military monster that is beyond the control of the military. They have changed the nature of warfare so much that the name "war" should no longer be used, but rather something like "mutual suicide" or "death trigger." Any cuts in nuclear weapons preparation, possession, or use make more sense and give more hope than depending upon them.

Argument 10. Saint Thomas Aquinas

Thomas Aquinas agreed that war is morally permissible in certain circumstances, and he was a great theologian. What about that? (Aquinas is highly esteemed among Catholic theologians because he was the first theologian to write a synthesis of Aristotelian philosophy and Christian theology. His twelfth-century compendium of theology is influential even today.)

Reply to "Saint Thomas Aquinas"

Yes, St. Thomas Aquinas agreed with the Just-Unjust War Theory of Augustine. If he were alive today and considered what nuclear weapons have done and can do, what technology has done to unite the world, what modern popes and church councils have said about all this, he might have led the way in discarding the theory (making *all* war and military action wrong).

In his own day Thomas didn't do much more than affirm the fourth-century opinions of Augustine. In his arguments he used the same texts and interpretations as Augustine, adding little or nothing of his own. It seems to me that he did not investigate the question himself. (The arguments showing the weaknesses of Augustine's theory are in chapter five.)

In answering his own question, "Is fighting war always a sin?" (*Summa Theologica* II-II, prologue and part of Art. 1) Thomas never cited the pacifist statements of the early Church Fathers. He also interpreted pacifist texts from the New Testament in a very narrow sense. For example, in dealing with Jesus' command to his would-be defender Peter, "Put up your sword ... all those who take the sword shall perish by the sword" (Mt. 26:52), Thomas limits the application of this text to those who "take the sword without official authorization." Thus, Jesus' statement is forced against the context to harmonize with Thomas' requirement that proper authority is needed to initiate warfare. The gospel, however, says that Jesus prohibits the act of using the sword. There is no reference to permission from authority (*Summa Theologica*, II-II, 40, 1 Obj. 1).

Two texts that forbid resistance to evil are given a meaning not warranted by their gospel context, and are interpreted by Thomas so as to limit and turn them around to fit into the Just-Unjust War Theory and come to mean almost the opposite of what they say. One example is Jesus' counsel in the Sermon on the Mount, "But I say this to you, offer the wicked man no resistance" (Mt. 5:39, JB). And Paul's, "Never repay evil with evil. . . . Never try to get revenge. Leave that . . . to God's anger" (Rom. 12:17-19, JB). Thomas limits the application of these texts to cases of self-defense involving no more than two private citizens. He denies that they apply to soldiers, or even to a civilian defending others besides oneself. How does he arrive at this conclusion? Where is his evidence?

Thomas goes further and says the texts do not apply to external acts, but only to the dispositions in the mind

(*Summa Theologica* II-II, 40, 1 Art. 2: 64-67, and Art. 5). Does this mean that I may kill a person as long as I don't intend to kill? May I drop an atom bomb that kills, and intend only defense, not killing? This is what Thomas seems to say. But he says it only about war. It should follow that I can commit adultery as long as I intend love and affection; idolatry, provided I intend only to please the devotées of a false god; and so on, with all sins. I cannot agree with Thomas on this, if this is his meaning. The commands of Jesus and Paul are turned around to allow the very violence that they forbid. When this has to be done to uphold a theory, it doesn't say much for the agreement of the theory with Scripture.

Thomas found direct support for warfare in judicial precepts of the Old Testament. In applying these to Christians in the New Testament, he ignored God's special use of warfare in the Old Testament and how that ceased to apply in the New Testament (see chapter four).

It is not surprising that Thomas repeated the Just-Unjust War tradition of Augustine. Thomas lived in the age of the Crusades, when popes were urging war.

Thomas's teacher, Albertus Magnus, was commissioned to preach a Crusade. Three of Thomas's blood brothers were soldiers. When Thomas is considered not only for his work, but in the context in which he lived, there is a wide divergence from the example of Jesus. The influence of fighting and conquest was strong. Culture and circumstance had much to do with shaping his acceptance of the war theory of Augustine. What he wrote showed little thought of his own. He uses no original texts, and merely copies Augustine.

Just as he accepted slavery, an almost unquestioned tradition in his day, so he accepted war. Had he lived in our age of nuclear weapons and production by machines in which slavery is no longer accepted, he might be the lead voice in explaining the evil of both slavery and war.

Why? Because he was an innovator and synthesizer in his day. He brought the works of Aristotle into harmony with Christian thought. Maybe if he lived today he would have synthesized technology and theology. We know only the Thomas of his age.

Both Augustine and Thomas lived at a time when the state religion of the Holy Roman Empire was Christianity. Aquinas taught that the state could burn heretics, for they constituted a grave danger to the highest good of its citizens, which was their Christian faith. Today we reject that teaching as wrong and unjust—a clear sign that Aquinas, too, in this, as well as in his treatment of the Just-Unjust War Theory, was a product of his age.

Argument 11. Obedience to Authority

Pacifists reject the authority of the state. This leads to anarchy and chaos. It is part of the social nature of humans that we must live together and that requires some sort of government authority.

Reply to "Obedience to Authority"

Pacifists respect authority, but they recognize a hierarchy of authority. When a civil command or law is not in conflict with divine law, it is to be obeyed. But when a civil command is in conflict with the divine law, it is not to be followed. Divine law takes precedence.

The pacifist does not oppose legitimate authority, but questions the legitimacy of the authority of the state to kill or to order its citizens to kill. No Christian can say to the state, "I will do anything you tell me to do, no matter what." The Christian's first duty is "Seek first the kingdom of God," as Jesus told us, or in the words of Peter, "We must obey God rather than man."

Every modern state, except India, was born in homicide, and they all continue to survive by threatening death to all who oppose them. The Christian attitude toward such an institution (that is, the state) should be a suspicious questioning of all that is commanded until the commands can be weighed in the light of conscience. When the orders are in accord with conscience, the Christian finds God's authority in legitimate authority. Where conscience objects to the order, the Christian obeys God rather than humans. In this sense the Christian is the "loving adversary" or "witness to truth" that helps the state become what it ought to be, the promoter of the common good for all.

Argument 12. Spiritual Values Need Defense

There are worse things than war and the taking of life. The destruction of spiritual values is one of them. These values must be defended. Pacifists lose sight of this.

First Reply to "Spiritual Values Need Defense"

Of course, spiritual values need to be defended. But if spiritual values are to be defended, the means used must be such that they do not destroy spiritual values. Defense must be by moral means. Pacifists argue that "killing people is not a moral means." The end does not justify the means. Defending spiritual values (a good end) does not justify using evil means (killing).

Second Reply to "Spiritual Values Need Defense"

Revolutionaries often argue that unjust tyrants need to

be overthrown, so they organize and kill the tyrant. In order to seize power they become unjust murderers. In the process of seeking justice, they act unjustly. One unjust tyrant has been substituted for another. Something similar happens when spiritual values are defended by killing. In the process of seeking to defend them, spiritual values are lost. Most Christian leaders under Hitler sought to protect spiritual values by going along with Hitler's wars. They would have defended spiritual values better by refusing to follow Hitler.

Third Reply to "Spiritual Values Need Defense"

The way to defend spiritual values is the way of Christ, of Gandhi, of Martin Luther King, Jr.—nonviolent resistance to evil. Christ did not kill or advise killing to spread his kingdom. The reason is that killing does not spread his kingdom. He taught us how to die for what we believe and not to kill for it. Gandhi applied the love-ethic of Jesus to national and international conflicts. He organized nonviolent resistance on a national scale to free more than four hundred million Indians from the domination of the British Empire. By these means he defended and even strengthened spiritual values. Martin Luther King, Jr. freed millions of American blacks from the worst features of legalized racism. Through his nonviolent national defense of blacks, he strengthened spiritual values of both whites and blacks.

Jesus taught us that by losing our lives, we save them. He gave us the example through his life and death of the way to do that. He defended spiritual values. Those who say that this is not an efficient way of doing things, that there is no chance of success without military defense, ought to ask themselves what they think of the cross? Was that efficient? Was that a successful defense of spiritual values?

Argument 13. Vatican Council II Allows for a War of Self-Defense

Some maintain that the second Vatican Council concluded that soldiers who engage in wars of self-defense can be viewed as instruments of peace.

Reply to "Vatican Council II's War of Self-Defense"

Vatican II never mentions the words "war" or "self-defense" in the context quoted. It speaks of "legitimate" defense as long as there is no world authority capable of maintaining peace. The entire section of Vatican II (*Church in the Modern World*) is introduced by a call for an entirely fresh and new evaluation of war because of the massive destructive power of new weapons.[27] It condemns the use of these weapons on whole areas and their peoples as crimes against God and humankind. Such a condemnation says that no theory that includes use of nuclear weapons be allowed. No self-defense that uses nuclear weapons is allowed.

Vatican II appeals to conscience. It calls on all military personnel to disobey for conscience' sake any orders that ask them to use weapons of mass destruction. It calls on all governments to respect in their laws those whose conscience forbids them to bear arms.

Vatican II calls on all nations to consider nonviolent means of defense as more in line with the gospel and more available to all nations, especially the weaker nations.

In the context of a condemnation of the use of nuclear weapons, and an appeal to conscience and nonviolence, and under severe pressure from a small number of bishops, Vatican II speaks of the "right to legitimate defense." No mention of the Just-Unjust War Theory is made, not even in a footnote. "War" is not mentioned either. In this context "legitimate" cannot mean use of nuclear defense. This is condemned. It seems also that any defense that risks nuclear war is not "legitimate." This would include any war by a nation that possesses nuclear weapons. It is not clear what defense could be legitimate. Nonviolent defense would be legitimate. In India, Gandhi used it successfully. In the United States, workers have formed unions to secure their rights. Martin Luther King organized boycotts as a means toward greater justice for blacks. Our government uses economic sanctions. All of this is legitimate.

The word "legitimate" in the Vatican II document was a compromise in a statement that is otherwise a clear call to peacemaking along the lines indicated. This wavering note of "legitimate defense" illustrates the failure of the council to rise to the vision of peace put before them in the letter of John XXIII, *Peace on Earth.*

Nonviolent defense certainly could and I think should be considered as a type of legitimate defense, and may have been what was in the minds of the drafters of the document. Nonviolent defense means resistance that is short of using violent force, and such actions include a wealth of opportunities that tend not to be considered by most national governments today. However, they are not unknown and include economic sanctions, such as those the U.S. has used with the Soviet Union in grain trade embargo.

But even with this failure or waffling, the council does not approve of the Just-Unjust War Theory, or of wars of self-defense. It talks about "legitimate" defense in a way that leaves open what kind of defense it considers legitimate, though it makes some kinds of defense clearly illegitimate.

To admit that no use of nuclear weapons is allowed and also maintain that it is morally permissible to manufacture and possess nuclear weapons without intent to use them, is the modern version of weighing how many angels can dance on the head of a pin. It is also a good illustration of how the Just-Unjust War Theory does not apply in the nuclear age.

Argument 14. Conscientious Objectors Are Cowards

Pacifists are cowards who are afraid to die. But there are worse evils than death, such as slavery, denial of freedom to worship God, and denial of other freedoms.

Reply to "Conscientious Objectors Are Cowards"

Conscientious objectors are no more afraid of death than anyone else. As one American soldier in Vietnam wrote to me, "I do not fear death. What I do fear is to die in the act of killing in a war that I believe is immoral." That states the difference between a pacifist and a soldier. The difference consists in a willingness to kill, or a refusal to kill.

To the argument "There are worse things than death," the conscientious objector replies, "Yes, I agree. Killing another, when I believe God forbids it, is worse." Death, slavery, and other physical evils cannot destroy my soul. Sin can and does. If the communists bomb us with nuclear weapons, they destroy our bodies. If we plan to use nuclear weapons on them, we destroy our souls even before we press the button.

Argument 15. Deterrence Works

If deterrence has worked for thirty-seven years, why abandon it? It has kept the peace and prevented nuclear war. What better alternative can the pacifist offer?

Reply to "Deterrence Works"

The argument presumes what is not true. Is it true that any major power has been stopped from anything they would otherwise have done because of the nuclear threat? That is only speculation. No one knows for sure. The Cuban missile crisis, despite the threats in the beginning, was finally resolved by negotiations, not by deterrence.

Three fallacies presumed true by the question are: Deterrence is a response to, rather than a cause of, our hostile world climate. Second, we have no other choice, even if we wanted to use one. Third, deterrence is a stable, static condition. Our acceptance of these and similar fallacies blocks us from a serious look at what deterrence is and what it does, and it leads us to a false trust in deterrence.

After thirty-seven years of deterrence, we are closer to nuclear war than we were when it started, and we are rushing toward war at a faster rate than ever before. We have 35,000 nuclear bombs today. At Hiroshima, we had two and the Soviets had none. Now, six or seven nations have nuclear bombs. Added to them President Ford said in 1976 "There are twenty others with the technical competence and the material to make them and by 1985 the figure will be approximately forty. A world of many nuclear weapon states' he notes, "could become extremely unstable and dangerous."

"In twenty years," asserts the Committee for Economic Development, a prestigious group of business leaders, "one hundred countries will possess the raw materials and the knowledge necessary to produce nuclear bombs." By the year 2000, it says 'the total plutonium expected to have been produced as a by-product of nuclear power would be equivalent in explosive potential to one million bombs of the size that destroyed Nagasaki."[27]

While the industrial nations spend six billion dollars a year on arms, the poor starve and grow in numbers. Instead of responding to this by stopping the mad race, we speed it up. In this way, both from the military point of view and from the economic point of view, deterrence fuels the arms race and works against the very peace it claims to produce.

Deterrence depends on a balance of terror between the U.S. and the USSR. Our push to get new and better weapons is designed to gain superiority over the USSR. The push leads to an imbalance in deterrence and threatens war.

To admit that no use of nuclear weapons is allowed and also maintain that it is morally permissible to manufacture and possess nuclear weapons without intent to use them, is the modern version of weighing how many angels can dance on the point of a needle. Deterrence includes within itself the taproot of the violence in our society: our intent to use nuclear weapons on people. This intent has corrupted the fiber of our moral life to such an extent that in the U.S. alone we have one and a quarter million abortions each year; violence and killing have become staple entertainment on our television screens; our prison population has doubled; and our military budget has more than tripled. All of this is linked to our acceptance of a deterrence policy which has at its heart our intent to use nuclear bombs on people.

It can be argued that the U.S. has used nuclear weapons other than the bombs dropped on Hiroshima and Nagasaki. During the fifties and the early sixties the U.S. used many bombs in nuclear weapon tests exposing U.S. soldiers to radiation. These tests were coordinated with foreign policy objectives in Korea and cold war diplomacy with the Soviet Union. Also, bombs have been used in diplomacy by threatening to use them at times of crisis, as in the beginning of the Cuban missile crisis in 1962.

Is this really use of nuclear weapons? Is it use of a gun when I hold the gun to another man's head when I ask him for money? Such threats have been used openly and secretly by all U.S. presidents since 1945, with the possible exception of President Ford.

The logic of deterrence would have us believe that there is no other choice, so therefore, there is no moral question about it, and no sin is committed. Why? Because following it is the only option. This silences the moral challenge so that deterrence has become accepted militarily and morally by some. If we accept this position as the only option we define peace as an ever increasing speeding to disaster during which we starve the poor, corrupt our moral lives, and leave God out of our plans. In accepting deterrence, we cut ourselves off from our moral roots in the Scriptures and make a mockery of the gospel. We trade our worship of the true God for a worship of gods of metal. Instead of living in peace with others, we make world relations a mutually hostage relationship.

Argument 16. We Are Not All Children of God
Pacifists say we are all children of God. We are not all children of God, and brothers and sisters to each other.

We become children of God by baptism. The unbaptized are not children of God.

Reply to "We Are Not All Children of God"

According to Catholic theology, the baptism of desire also makes one a child of God. Baptism of desire is the desire to do all that God wants one to do. It includes the implicit desire for baptism where water baptism is impossible. This is the way Catholic theologians answer the question "What happens to good people who live a good life and die a good death but have never heard about Jesus or about baptism?" Without this answer, God would not be seen as just, because God would be keeping good people out of heaven without any fault on their part. This does away with the exclusionist viewpoint held by some Christians. No one is excluded from salvation just because they haven't heard about Jesus or baptism.

We are all children of God by creation, conservation, and by redemption. We are all created by God, and all that God made is good (Gen. 1). Jesus tells us (all of us) to say to God, "Our Father." Jesus said, "Whatsoever you do to the least of my little ones, you do unto Me." How could that be true if we were not all God's children?

We are all God's children by conservation. God sustains our existence. We are also God's children by redemption. Jesus came to redeem all. He is the universal savior. He didn't come just for one people. Just as in creation, God's redemptive grace is magnanimous. God's gift of sonship and daughtership is unlimited.

Do you have to be baptized to go to heaven? What is Jesus' view of this from the cross? To the repentant thief, Jesus promised paradise.

This idea of the inherent goodness in each person is the

theme of Pope John XXIII's great encyclical letter, *Peace on Earth*. Humans are not evil. The idea that people are evil and are rescued from that evil by Jesus coming down on earth is not the Catholic view. The Catholic view is not that we are evil but are saved by Christ's blood that is thrown over us as a cloak to protect our evil from the just judgment. Evil, in the Catholic view, is the absence of a perfection that should be there. Evil is not something in itself but the absence of a good which should be present. What should be present is the integrity of our nature so that all our senses and desires be under the control of and subordinate to our reason. But that subordination was broken by original sin. In that sense we have fallen from God's grace and need baptism to regain it. Baptism restores us fallen humans to the state of grace lost by our first parents. We become children of God by a visible sign of God's grace, baptism. Thus we become God's children by baptism although by creation we already were God's children. How can this be? It is mysterious! Vatican Council II calls the church "the mystery of the people of God." God is mysterious. It follows that all our relations to God, if we search deeply enough, are mysterious. For example, how can I be both a child of God and a sinner? Yet I am. How can a person be a child of God and an atheist?

A human analogy may help. An atheist is like a child who is separated from his father at an early age so that he never knows his father. We still say that he is a child of his father even if he does not know or recognize his father. We would consider his statement wrong if he said, "I have no father." Likewise, a sinner is like a child who refuses to obey his father and leaves home to live in sin. He is disobedient, sinful, rebellious, but still a child of his father. His return to the father through repentance is like being born again. In a sense he is "born again" because he recognizes who he is and has a new life of closer unity with God.

Are not the righteous separated from the unrighteous along the lines of Matthew 25 and not simply by being Christian in name only (see Mt. 7:21)? Yes, God will separate the sheep and the goats at the last judgment, but that judgment is done by God. We don't have the wisdom to make that judgment. Moreover, we are told, "Judge not." So the fact that we believe that God will judge in the future doesn't help us much here and now to decide who is responding to God's call and who is not.

Thus in many ways we can be and are God's children because we are related to God in many ways: creation, redemption, baptism, obedience, faith, repentance.

The Society of Friends seem to recognize this when they say, "There is that of God in every person." The importance for Christians of accepting as broadly as possible a definition of children of God is illustrated by the failure to recognize which it has led to wars among religious sects. This idea that we don't understand other people and their relation to God is illustrated by God's complaint to the Jewish people that he doesn't want their sacrifices if they are going to fight with each other, and if they are going to be unjust to each other. "Do you think I want these sacrifices? I have more than enough of the sheep you burn" (Is. 1, v. 11). The sacrifice that God wanted was that people care for each other, care for the widowed, and the weak and the oppressed. "Let justice and mercy flow like rivers; that is the true worship of the Lord" (Is. 1:10-20). This shows God as caring for all of us as the Father of us all. This idea of God's universal fatherhood/

motherhood is a thread which ties together the theology of creation, redemption, sacraments, original sin, and love.

Seen in this light, the peace issue is central to Christian theology, not peripheral or marginal. Peace defined as "reconciliation with God, my Father, and my human brothers and sisters" is so close to love itself, that it is almost the same as the doctrine of love.

All Christian theology is so affected by what we say about peace because peace is the prelude to and companion to love. It follows that the theology of peace must be taught, believed, and practiced at the risk of distorting every aspect of faith.

How can we believe all the ramifications of the incarnation: God with us in human form, all of us related to Jesus as brothers and sisters, God dwelling in us through grace, all of us loved personally by God as shown in Jesus. How can we believe all this, and then use weapons of mass destruction to kill? How can we believe that we are all one body, united in Christ, and also believe we can kill each other on government orders? How can we believe that each one of us is precious in God's sight and be ready or even preparing to kill each other on government orders?

If we cannot believe that killing is wrong because of our faith, a common sense look at the lethal technology of our nuclear age will teach us that same lesson. The realistic alternative of our times is that we must cooperate together or perish together in the flames of our planet.

Our hope cannot be in weapons, in gods of metal. In that way lies death. God offers us the choice of life or death. Both faith and technology make it clear that we must choose life for others, too, as well as for ourselves. If we choose to kill, we will certainly write our own death sentence for this world and, unless we repent, for the next.

With God's help we do not need to choose death or killing. We can depend on God to help us if we trust in God—not in weapons of death. Pope John XXIII in his final letter, *Peace on Earth,* asks every believer to be a little light. "Every believer in this world of ours must be a spark of light, a center of love, a vivifying leaven. This is the peace which we implore of him with the ardent yearning of our every prayer."

CHAPTER SEVEN

The U.S. Bishops and the Bomb

Before the pastoral was issued, Bishop Walter Sullivan of Richmond, Virginia said, "I could save the bishops a whole lot of time, and a whole lot of energy, if they would just say, 'No Nukes. No to their use, no to their manufacture, and no to their possession.' "

That's true. It would have saved them time, but it would have eliminated the three-year process in which the American Catholic bishops educated themselves. They brought the whole world into dialogue on the issue, and roused other conferences of bishops around the world to make their own statements. Even if they could have gotten together and agreed to Bishop Sullivan's formula, it might not have been wise to do so because of all of the benefits coming from the dialogue during the formulation of the four drafts, and the 40,000-word final statement.

If the issues were as clear as Bishop Sullivan wanted, the bishops' Peace Pastoral might simply be brushed aside by Catholic officers in the Pentagon, and even by the majority of American Catholics. It can't be brushed aside quickly now, because it takes too long to read. It can't be brushed aside quickly because it was flashed across the world by an aggressive U.S. press. I attended almost all of the bishop's meetings on the Peace Pastoral. There were more press accredited to the meetings than there were bishops attending. During press conferences after each session, the row of television cameras across the hotel ballroom made it difficult for many reporters to see the speaker. Press coverage from Europe, Asia, and South America grew larger each year. It can't be brushed aside quickly because much worldwide attention has been focused on it. It won't be brushed aside quickly because the topic is vitally important to everyone.

I will treat four components of the pastoral: first, the context in which it was written; second what it says; third, what it fails to say; and fourth, what its implications are for us.

The Context

The importance of the letter may be understood from the fact that this was the first time in 2,000 years that any national group of Catholic bishops talked about the morality of war and peace. This letter breaks that silence with three years of open discussion. Open discussion of the issue may be the most important thing that was done. As in the struggle against racial injustice, open discussion is half of the victory; so it is with militarism. Neither look good when the clear light of truth reveals them for what they are.

Before Vatican Council II (1963-1965), no general council of the church had ever talked about the morality of war. That was the first time a council had officially declared anything about war. This statement of the U.S. bishops builds on Vatican II and goes beyond it both in extending and applying that teaching. The fact, also, that the letter was issued by the bishops belonging to a world superpower representing 52 million Catholics gave it added significance.

Much of the history that preceded this pastoral and helped shape it is given in *The Bishops and the Bomb* (see bibliography). The pastoral developed in this way. At the 1980 yearly meeting of bishops, Bishop Thomas Gumbleton of Detroit and Bishop Frank Murphy of Baltimore asked the assembly: "Do we believe that the peace message of Jesus is being heard in our council of government? Do we have answers to the question of our people on the nuclear issue? Should we not do something about it?" They received a standing ovation. Archbishop John Roach of Minneapolis-St. Paul, chair of the conference, chose Archbishop Joseph Bernardin, former chair of the conference, to head a committee to formulate and develop the first draft. Bernardin, who had a reputation for ability to build a consensus, chose one bishop with a high public profile on peacemaking, Bishop Gumbleton, and another with a high association with the military, Bishop John O'Connor, formerly an admiral and chief of chaplains. To represent the moderate opinion of most other bishops, after consultation, he chose Bishop Fulcher, auxiliary of Columbus, and Bishop Reilly of Norwich. With staff help and interviews over three years, input was received from experts in theology, nuclear physics, the military, government, peace activists, and nuclear engineers. All of the bishops helped to form the document by written comments and discussions at their regular annual meeting.

Some of the texts of Old and New Testament writings that influenced the bishops are set forth in the beginning of the letter. I have mentioned some of them in chapters one and four. These are some of the influences which brought the Catholic Church out of 1,600 years of silence about, or acceptance of war.

What the Pastoral Letter Says

Now we take a look at what the pastoral says. First of all, it reaffirms the nonviolence of the first three hundred years of Christianity as a viable option for Catholic Christians and for all Christians. If anyone now says that because of the gospel I cannot take part in killing, then let everyone know that such a person is following a very old tradition of the Catholic Church. Affirming this is a major statement.

A sample of its impact came to me through a student at Georgetown who said that two years ago he refused to register. His parents didn't like it; they said he had disgraced the family and they urged him to register. He told me, "Now I just say to them: 'See what the bishops said! Now I'll never register, I feel stronger than ever.' "

In the United States Catholics have made a big point of proving their patriotism. One of the ways we do this is to put the names of the war dead on plaques in the back of the church. We should now begin also inscribing on those plaques the names of those who refused, for conscience' sake, to be a part of war.

Another thing that the pastoral says is that, although there is a Just War Theory (they enumerated seven conditions to be fulfilled for the war to be just), they said that this theory cannot be used in the nuclear age to support a nuclear war. Neither the gospel nor the Just War Theory approve of nuclear war. Both condemn it. Two basic requirements of this theory—protection of the innocent and "proportionality" (more good than evil must result from the war)—cannot be fulfilled. The pastoral says that there are only two ways in which Christians have tried to relate faith to war. One way is the gospel of nonviolence and the other is the Just War Theory. Both of them say "No" to nuclear war. This is the basic message of the pastoral.

The bishops go on to talk about the nuclear age and nuclear warfare. They say that no Catholic can be a part of nuclear war. In doing this they repeated what Vatican II had said, "The destruction of entire cities or extensive areas with their populations is a crime against God and man. It merits unequivocal and unhesitating condemnation."[26] That was the basic statement that guided the U.S. bishops in condemning participation in nuclear war. In line with that, they repeated what the bishops in the United States had said in 1976 in their pastoral *To Live in Christ Jesus:* "Not only is it wrong to attack civilian populations but it is also wrong to threaten to attack them as part of a strategy of deterrence." That is the second assertion that they made—that the intention to wage nuclear war is immoral. In saying this, they were only repeating traditional morality that says that which is wrong to do is wrong to intend to do. "If it is wrong for me to kill you, it is wrong for me to intend to kill you." They were applying this to the nuclear age. In saying this, they went beyond Vatican II.

Vatican II didn't formally deal with intention. Intention was brought up at the council but never explicitly condemned on the grounds that it is always wrong to intend to do what it is wrong to do. The council's condemnation of nuclear war implied the condemnation of intending to make nuclear war; they didn't clearly say it though. The bishops of the United States did say it.

Further, in view of the fact that it is wrong to use nuclear weapons because of the massive destructive capacities of these weapons, so it is also wrong to target them on cities. Then, after consultation with experts of all kinds, they concluded that such targeting on industrial or military targets within cities would kill so many civilians that it could never be allowed. When this point was discussed one of the bishops who had been a paratrooper chaplain argued, "If you say that we cannot target a city, the enemy could put their guns in the city, and if you can't destroy those guns, even if you have to destroy the city, then you are going to lose the war." What that kind of argument did was to illustrate how the Just War Theory does not work in the nuclear age. The bishops rejected the argument.

In line with their basic stand, "No nuclear war," the bishops also ruled out "first use" of nuclear weapons. The U.S. asserts that in certain circumstances we will use nuclear weapons first. This is also NATO policy.

In line with their basic stand, "No nuclear war," massive retaliation, even after we are hit, is found to be contrary to morality.

When you put all this together—no war, no intent to use nuclear weapons, no city or strategic targeting, no first use, and no retaliation—what you have is a statement of nuclear pacifism. This is a new term for morality and for moral theology. Nuclear pacifism's most basic meaning is that nuclear war and all that leads to it is immoral.

The pastoral letter comments on new U.S. missile systems like the MX, the Trident submarine, and the cruise missiles. These systems are viewed as an escalation of the arms race to which the bishops say "Halt." Because of that, they question the United States' deterrence policy. They condemn a deterrence policy which escalates the arms race or is aimed at superiority over the Soviet

Union, or preparation for nuclear war. The pastoral challenges U.S. foreign and military policy. It calls the individual to follow his or her conscience. It calls the military person, the working person, the citizen, the teacher, the religious educator, bishops, and beyond that the world in general, to turn away from worshiping gods of metal, and look to the living God for security.

In a world where nuclear missiles have made national defense impossible, the bishops call for support of the United Nations or the development of a world authority that could insure peace. They see the U.N. as the prime candidate to fulfill this task.

What the Pastoral Letter Fails to Say

The bishops' letter doesn't say that it's a sin to build nuclear weapons, but it does say that it's wrong to use them. Now compare that with the bishops' statement on abortion. The bishops say that abortion is wrong. It is wrong to have an abortion, it's wrong to be a part of an abortion, it's wrong to build an abortion clinic, and so on. The whole thing is consistent. But on the nuclear issue, they stop short.

They say in the pastoral that there is need for a continuing critical evaluation of American policy, but they give no norms on how to make this evaluation: which missile systems, what program, or how many weapons need to be examined. Cardinal Krol, speaking for the bishops before the Armed Services Committee, said that if it becomes clear that we are not using our deterrence to move toward disarmament, then Catholic theology will have to turn around and be in complete opposition. It will have to say that there is no possibility of possession of the weapons.

Cardinal Bernardin, in a press conference at one of the meetings was asked, "Are not the bishops ambiguous on the issue of deterrence?" He answered, "Yes." The reporters laughed. He continued, "We structured ambiguity into this. We knew that we were not going to completely outlaw every kind of deterrence. We are going to say that some sort of limited deterrence is allowed, so how do you allow for that and not have ambiguity? If you say that you can't have a nuclear war, then you can't intend a nuclear war, but deterrence includes the threat to use. So, how can you have deterrence?"

The bishops noted that in deterrence there are sinful elements: first, possession of weapons which cannot be used; second, intention to use the weapons which is part of deterrence policy; third, fueling of the arms race through deterrence; fourth, the possibility of accidental war due to the presence of the weapons, and fifth, the possibility that deterrence will not work.

They said that our intention to use nuclear weapons is at the heart of our deterrence policy. They also saw that it's bad morality and bad theology to approve of a means that you cannot use, or approve of getting a goal by an evil means. By approving deterrence, it seemed that they approved of getting peace by threatening destruction, a destruction which is already declared immoral. Such an approval would be sinful.

The bishops were concerned that deterrence fuels the arms race. The pope's frequent statements and the facts on hunger and arms spending were clear on these points. Fifty thousand people starve to death each day (worldwide) while the world spends $1.3 billion per day on armaments. Even with all that spending (which is a major cause of massive global starvation), there is no assurance that, even with deterrence, we will avoid war.

They saw all of these sinful elements, but they saw a good element in deterrence also. It seems, in the view of some people, to be a way of preventing nuclear war for the time being. The bishops quoted a statement of Pope John Paul which said that deterrence that is based on balance—certainly not as an end in itself, but as a step on the way to progressive disarmament—may be judged as morally acceptable.

To reconcile these two apparently contradictory statements, "one centimeter" of use of nuclear weapons had to be somehow allowed—not nuclear war nor the intent to make nuclear war—but maybe in a theoretic-type of deterrence which exists only on paper or in the mind. But this would look foolish if said too clearly, so it was done by "structured ambiguity."

What they ended up with was two kinds of deterrence: first, a deterrence which does not include "use," a deterrence which does not include "intention to use," a deterrence which leads to necessary disarmament. That is the kind of deterrence that is approved. They do not tell us where to find such a policy, or even if it exists.

The second kind of deterrence is the type practiced by the U.S. and the USSR. It includes the intent to use nuclear weapons, first-strike capability, massive retaliation, and readiness for nuclear war.

The bishops do not clearly say that the U.S. deterrence policy is immoral. They don't clearly say that the deterrence approved is not U.S. deterrence. They don't say clearly that the deterrence that is approved is found nowhere except on paper or in the mind. They leave that ambiguous. Through ambiguity, they avoid contradicting themselves. They also blur the message.

Why was this "structured ambiguity" put in? To allow for both the statements of Vatican Council II that condemns nuclear war, and the statement of John Paul II allowing some sort of limited deterrence. They settled on a theoretical deterrence.

Further, the bishops never talked about why people go to war. Some go for vanity and glory; others because they are mislead by past wars or false promises. They do it, in American slang, "to be a man." To be a man is to be a soldier. The bishops don't mention the morality of this with regard to God's call to us to be peacemakers.

They also did not tell the chaplains, who are under their charge, that they must instruct all of the men to not torture prisoners, that they cannot be a part of the nuclear program, and that they cannot be a part of the preparation for nuclear programs. One of the bishops in the discussion said, "Do you realize that if we put this program in and say there can be no nuclear war and that there can be no intention to use nuclear weapons, that we are asking all of the military officers who are a part of that to stop their jobs?" He was right. By implication they are asking this. By implication they are asking the chaplains to do this, but they don't clearly say so.

They didn't say anything about paying for war through taxes, either. This implication is clearly what Archbishop Raymond Hunthausen took from it. If it is wrong to use nuclear weapons, then if I give the government money on my behalf to go ahead and manufacture them, am I not doing wrong? They didn't say that.

They didn't say that it's wrong to work in a nuclear plant. They didn't go as far as Bishop Leroy Matthiesen of Amarillo, Texas, who advised that no one should work in a plant which makes nuclear weapons.

The Implications for Us

The letter gives much pastoral advice to educators, priests, citizens, workers in arms factories, and men and women in the military, but it fails to say that young men asked to join an army planning to use nuclear weapons should refuse to go. Yet, all of this and more is implied by what the bishops do say.

Perhaps they did not wish to crush the bruised reed; perhaps they could not get consensus for anything more than they finally said (the final draft was approved by a vote of 238 to 9). Perhaps they believed that a developed conscience aided by the Holy Spirit would overcome the deficiencies in their message.

Whatever they thought, their letter was a giant step forward in helping Christians begin to understand the relation of their faith to making war, especially nuclear war.

They did unveil the fiction of the union of church and state in the United States. They said that the church has something to say even if the state doesn't like it. They also issued a call—it wasn't as clear and it wasn't as sharp as it could have been—but it was a strong call to conscience on the issue of war and peace.

The pastoral brings the church of today in the United States into a head-on confrontation with the God of Sodom and Gomorrah. Remember the story of Sodom and Gomorrah: God had decided that the cities of Sodom and Gomorrah were so evil, sick, and corrupt that they needed to be destroyed. And he told his servant Abraham that he was planning to do that. Then Abraham argued and negotiated with God and said, "If I find ten just people, will you relent?" And God said, "All right, find them." He found Lot and his wife and their two children and their wives. Six people were all that he could find, but God negotiated even after he had set his intention to destroy. That sets an example for us today in our world of nuclear danger.

Only a few more may be needed, they may be three or four people reading this book, three or four people in the Pentagon, three or four people in the arms business— people who will listen to God's call and turn away from worshiping gods of metal and begin to worship the true God. Turn away and stop contributing to the disaster which faces us.

The bishops end with a message of hope. They call their letter "The Challenge of Peace: God's Promise and Our Response." They define hope as the "capacity to live with danger without being overwhelmed by it." It is the ability to struggle against obstacles even when they appear insurmountable. That's a good definition of hope.

Augustine said "faith only tells us that there is a God, love tells us God is good, but hope tells us God will work God's will." He goes on to say, "Hope has two lovely daughters, anger and courage: anger so that what must not be will not be, and courage so that what must be will be." The point that Augustine makes is that we should have comfort, that we should not despair, that we need only a few. A few to be of good heart and a few to hope and put their faith in God. For hope that is strengthened by divine power is stronger than the bomb. Only a few are needed to make the choice—a few to add to those who are already doing something. And for those few here or wherever they are, I wish them anger and courage.

Notes

1. Refer to chapter 6 ("Argument: We Are Not All Children of God") for a fuller development of this important topic.

2. G.H.C., Macgregor, *The New Testament Basis of Pacifism*, p. 98.

3. Mark Twain, "War Prayer."

4. M. Gandhi, *Young India*, 1924. While it may seem unusual to some readers to bring those who don't use the Bible as their holy book—such as Mark Twain or Gandhi—into a discussion of the New Testament, it may indeed help the discussion by giving a biblical argument more meaning. Also, it may indicate that had Christians given a better example of following the New Testament instead of making war, world leaders like these two might have been Christians. On the evil of making war both of them are clear and forceful; they both agree with the New Testament, in contrast to many Christians.

5. This interpretation is that of John K. Stoner, Akron, Pa., who shared it with me in personal correspondence.

6. Macgregor, op. cit., p. 71.

7. Macgregor, ibid., p. 88.

8. Harnack, *Milita Christi*, p. 47.

9. J. H. Oldham, *Church, Community and State*, p. 19.

10. Millard C. Lind, *Yahweh Is a Warrior*

11. Jacob J. Enz, *The Christian and Warfare*, p. 49.

12. Texts ordering extermination of prisoners are Num. 33:1-17; Deut. 20:13-18; Josh. 8:22-24; Judg. 21:10; and 1 Sam. 15:3.

13. Roland Bainton, *Christian Attitudes Toward War and Peace*, p. 73.

14. John Ferguson, *Politics of Love*, p. 63.

15. Ferguson, ibid., p. 64.

16. Ferguson, ibid., p. 65.

17. *Five Classic Just War Theories*, University Microfilms, Ann Arbor, Michigan, 1971.

18. Kennedy, The Church and War, A Catholic Study, 1928.

19. Gordon Zahn, *German Catholics and Hitler's Wars*, 1969.

20. Council Daybook, Washington: United States Catholic Conference, 1965, I, 315; II, 172.

21. Gordon Zahn, "The Christian Vocation of Peace," *Ave Maria* May 23, 1968, p. 6.

22. *Catholic Standard and Times*, Philadelphia, August 14, 1969.

23. Reinhold Niebuhr, *Why the Christian Church Is Not Pacifist*, p. 15.

24. Niebuhr, ibid., p. 16.

25. John Howard Yoder, *What Would You Do?* Scottdale, Pa.: Herald Press, 1984. His entire book gives an in-depth answer to this question.

26. Yoder, ibid.

27. Sidney Lens, *The Day Before Doomsday*, pp. 218-219, Vatican II, *Constitution on Church in the Modern World*, par. 80.

Bibliography

Aldridge, Robert C., *The Counterforce Syndrome*, A Guide to
U.S. Nuclear Weapons and Strategic Doctrine, Transnational Institute, Washington, D.C., 1978. The author
spent 16 years with Lockheed as a missile designer.

Bainton, Ronald H., *Christian Attitudes Toward War and
Peace*, Abingdon Press, N.Y., 1960. History of shifting attitudes. Excellent.

Cadeaux, Cecil J., *The Early Church and the World*, Clark
Pub. Co., Edinburgh, 1925.

Caldicott, Dr. Helen, *Nuclear Madness*, Bantam Books, New
York, 1978.

Castelli, Jim, *The Bishops and the Bomb*, Image Books, New
York, 1983.

Douglass, James, *The Non-Violent Cross*, Macmillan, New
York, 1968.

Durland, William, *No King but Caesar*, A Catholic Lawyer
Looks at Christian Violence, Herald Press, Scottdale, Pa.,
1975.

Enz, Jacob J., *The Christian and Warfare*, The Roots of Pacifism in the Old Testament, Herald Press, Scottdale, Pa.,
1972.

Fahey, Joseph, *Justice and Peace*, Orbis Press, Maryknoll, N.Y.,
1979.

Ferguson, John, *Politics of Love*, The New Testament and
Non-Violent Revolution, Jas. Clarke Publishers,
Cambridge, England.

Grannis, Chris; Laffin, Arthur; and Schade, Elin, *The Risk of
the Cross*, Seabury Press, New York, 1981.

Ground Zero (Roger Molander), *Nuclear War: What's in It for
You?* Pocket Books, New York, 1982.

Hiatt, Dr. Howard, "No Effective Aid Exists for Nuclear Survivors," *New Haven Register*, Aug. 19, 1980.

King-Hall, Stephen, *Defense in the Nuclear Age*, Fellowship Publications, Nyack, N.Y. A military man's view of the nuclear age.

Lamoreau, John, and Beebe, Ralph, *Waging Peace: A Study in Biblical Pacifism*, Barclay Press, 1980. Examines Christ's teachings about violence and the response of the Christian church through its history.

Lasserre, Jean, *War and the Gospel*, Herald Press, Scottdale, Pa., 1962. One of the very few full-length books (244 pages) on the theology of peace. Good bibliography.

Lens, Sidney, *Day Before Doomsday*, Doubleday, Garden City, N.Y., 1977. Nuclear weapons, their danger, and what they can do.

Lind, Millard C., *Yahweh Is a Warrior*, The Theology of Warfare in Ancient Israel, Herald Press, Scottdale, Pa., 1980.

Macgregor, G. H. C., *The New Testament Basis of Pacifism*, Fellowship Publications, Nyack, N.Y. 1971.

Merton, Thomas, *Faith and Violence*, Notre Dame University Press, South Bend, Ind., 1968.

_____, *Thomas Merton on Peace*, edited by Gordon Zahn, McCall Pub. Co., New York, 1975.

NISBCO, *Words of Conscience*, Washington, D.C. Religious statements on conscientious objection from 79 religious groups; history of conscientious objection in the U.S. and statements by individuals.

Orr, Edgar W., *Christian Pacifism*, C. W. Daniel Co., Ashingdon, Rochford, Essex, England, 1957. Good bibliography.

Rutenber, Culbert, *The Dagger and the Cross*, Fellowship Publications, Nyack, N.Y., 1958.

Schell, Jonathan, *The Fate of the Earth*, Knopf, New York, 1982.

Sider, Ronald, and Taylor, Richard K., *Nuclear Holocaust and Christian Hope*, InterVarsity Press, Downers Grove, Ill., 1982.

Steiner, Susan Clemmer, *Joining the Army That Sheds No Blood*, Herald Press, Scottdale, Pa., 1982. Written for young people considering conscientious objection.

Strattman, Franziscus, *The Church and War, A Catholic Study*, Kennedy, N.Y., 1928.

Vanderhaar, Gerry, *Christians and Nonviolence in the Nuclear Age*, Twenty-Third Publications, Mystic, Conn., 1982.

Walters, Leroy, *Five Classic Just-War Theories*, University Microfilms, Ann Arbor, Michigan, 1971.

Windass, Stanley, *Christianity Versus Violence*, Sheed and Ward, London, 1964.

Yoder, John H., *Nevertheless*, Varieties of Religious Pacifism, Herald Press, Scottdale, Pa., 1971.

——————, *Politics of Jesus*, Eerdmans, Grand Rapids, Mich., 1972.

——————, *What Would You Do?* Herald Press, Scottdale, Pa., 1984.

Zahn, Gordon, *In Solitary Witness*, Holt, Rinehart, and Winston, New York, 1965. The life of Franz Jagerstatter, conscientious objector to Hitler's wars.

——————, *War, Conscience and Dissent*, Hawthorne Books, New York, 1967.

Index

A

Ahab, 62
Alfrink, Cardinal, 98
Andropov, Yuri, 16
Aquinas, Thomas, 85, 124
Ark of the Covenant, 62
Assyrians, 58, 59
Augustine, 82, 114, 124, 152

B

Bainton, Roland H., 73
Barman Resolution, 98
Barth, Karl, 98
Bernardin, Joseph, 143, 148

C

Cadeaux, Cecil, 81
Caesar, 43ff, 50, 51, 52
Caldicott, Helen, 89
Carter, President, 88
Catholic Worker, 29, 44
Cicero, 110
Clement of Alexandria, 70
Constantine, 78, 81
Cranston, Alan, 88
Cyprian, 72

D

Damascus, Pope, 77
Day, Dorothy, 29, 44
Diocletian, 75
Dion, 75
Douglass, James, 98

E

Eisenhower, President, 94

F

Ferguson, John, 73, 74, 98
Finn, Jim, 94
Fox, George, 79
Francis of Assisi, 79

G

Galerius, 75
Gandhi, 28, 74, 79, 113, 121, 129,
     131
Gentili, 85
Gideon, 60, 61
Grotius, 85
Gumbleton, Thomas, 143

H

Hannan, Philip, 91
Harnack, 51
Hiroshima, 117
Hunthausen, Raymond, 150

I

Isaiah, 58

J

Jeremiah, 58
John Paul II, 67, 149, 150
John XXIII, 95, 98, 136, 140
Justin, 69

K

Kennedy, John F., 87
King-Hall, General Stephen, 111,
     121, 122
King, Jr., Martin Luther, 79, 113,
     121, 129, 131

Krol, Cardinal John, 147

L
Lactanitius, 73
Lasserre, Jean, 98
Leviticus, 54
Lind, Millard, 98

M
Macgregor, G.H.C., 73, 98
Magnus, Albertus, 126
Marafini, Giuseppe, 98
Marcus Aurelius, 69
Matthiesen, Leroy, 150
Maximillian, 75
Mercier, Cardinal, 92
Micaiah, 62
Midian, 60
Moses, 56, 57
Murphy, Frank, 143

N
Nagasaki, 117
Nathan, 57
Niebuhr, Reinhold, 109
Nixon, Richard, 86

O
Oppenheimer, Robert, 67
Origen, 70
Orr, Edgar, 98

P, Q
Pacem in Terris, 89, 136, 140
Paul VI, Pope, 98
Penn, William, 79
Philistines, 62

R
Reagan, Ronald, 15
Roach, Archbishop John, 143
Ryan, S.J., Edward, 74

S
Sagan, Carl, 88
Schell, Jonathan, 88
Sider, Ronald, 98
Simons, Menno, 79
Solomon, 63
Stratman, Fraziscus, 85
Stonier, Tom, 87
Suarez, 85
Sullivan, Walter, 141

T
Taylor, Richard, 98
Tertullian, 35, 72
Theresa, Mother, 28
Tolstoy, Leo, 79
Trocmé, André, 98
Twain, Mark, 27

V
Vatican Council II, 79, 95, 97, 130, 131, 142, 145
Vitoria, 85

W
Waldensians, 79
Waters, Leroy, 85

Y
Yoder, John Howard, 98

Z
Zahn, Gordon, 98

Like most others active in the U.S. peace movement, Dick McSorley began in the civil rights struggle, first as pastor of an integrated congregation in St. James Church, southern Maryland, then as a marcher and follower of Martin Luther King, Jr., and Dan Berrigan, S.J. When they questioned the morality of the Vietnam War, he began to look into it and found that, like racism, it could not stand moral scrutiny. In 1965 he started a course in war and peace at Georgetown University that continues today and is always overcrowded.

Born in Philadelphia, the second of fifteen children, he entered the Jesuit order at age seventeen. Part of his training took him to the Philippine Islands to teach. There he became a war prisoner of the Japanese from December 13, 1941 to February 23, 1945.

Upon return to the States he was ordained a Catholic priest and began a teaching career at Scranton University. Currently he teaches and directs the Interdisciplinary Peace Studies Program at Georgetown University, Washington, D.C.

His experience with racism and militarism convinced him that they are intimately related and both immoral. They are both based on the same theology that we are not all brothers and sisters under the one God, that some people are better than (superior to) others. Both appeal to Scripture to try to justify themselves. Both appeal to nationalism and the same kind of specious arguments to support their stand. Would you like your daughter to marry a Negro? What would you do if a bandit tried to rape your mother? The parallel is comprehensive and deep.

McSorley sees militarism and racism as blood brothers. The militaristic side of this parallel is examined in this book.

OTHER BOOKS BY RICHARD McSORLEY

Kill? For Peace?
Killing people, particularly with nuclear weapons will not solve our problems. The book considers the moral implications of a nation basing its hopes for the future on vast and complicated plans to kill on a broad scale, particularly in light of the gospel teaching of love.

Peace Eyes
An account of journeys to five continents visiting peace communities and peace leaders. The reader shares in the peace process through the vision of peacemakers.

Both books are available from the Center for Peace Studies, Georgetown University, Washington, D.C. 20057. 202/625-4240

The Christian Peace Shelf

The Christian Peace Shelf is a selection of Herald Press books and pamphlets devoted to the promotion of Christian peace principles and their applications. The editor (appointed by the Mennonite Central Committee Peace Section) and an inter-Mennonite editorial board represent the historic concern for peace within these constituencies.

FOR SERIOUS STUDY

Durland, William R. *No King but Caesar?* (1975). A Catholic lawyer looks at Christian violence.

Enz, Jacob J. *The Christian and Warfare* (1972). The roots of pacifism in the Old Testament.

Hershberger, Guy F. *War, Peace, and Nonresistance* (third edition, 1969). A classic comprehensive work on nonresistance in faith and history.

Hornus, Jean-Michel. *It Is Not Lawful for Me to Fight* (1980). Early Christian attitudes toward war, violence, and the state.

Kaufman, Donald D. *What Belongs to Caesar?* (1969). Basic arguments against voluntary payment of war taxes.

Lasserre, Jean. *War and the Gospel* (1962). An analysis of Scriptures related to the ethical problem of war.

Lind, Millard C. *Yahweh Is a Warrior* (1980). The theology of warfare in ancient Israel.

Ramseyer, Robert L. *Mission and the Peace Witness* (1979). Implications of the biblical peace testimony for the evangelizing mission of the church.

Trocmé, André, *Jesus and the Nonviolent Revolution* (1975). The social and political relevance of Jesus.

Yoder, John H. *Nevertheless* (1971). The varieties and shortcomings of Christian pacifism.

_____, *The Original Revolution* (1972). Essays on Christian pacifism.

FOR EASY READING

Beachey, Duane. *Faith in a Nuclear Age* (1983). A Christian response to war.

Drescher, John M. *Why I Am a Conscientious Objector* (1982). A personal summary of basic issues for every Christian facing military involvements.

Eller, Vernard. *War and Peace from Genesis to Revelation* (1981). Explores peace as a consistent theme developing throughout the Old and New Testaments.

Kaufman, Donald D. *The Tax Dilemma: Praying for Peace, Paying for War* (1978). Biblical, historical, and practical considerations on the war tax issue.

Kraybill, Donald B. *Facing Nuclear War* (1982). A plea for Christian witness.

_____ *The Upside-Down Kingdom* (1978). A study of the synoptic Gospels on affluence, war-making, status-seeking, and religious exclusivism.

McSorley, Richard. *New Testament Basis of Peacemaking* (1985). A Jesuit makes the case for biblical pacifism.

Miller, John W. *The Christian Way* (1969). A guide to the Christian life based on the Sermon on the Mount.

Miller, Melissa, and Phil M. Shenk. *The Path of Most Resistance* (1982). Stories of Mennonite conscientious objectors who did not cooperate with the Vietnam draft.

Sider, Ronald J. *Christ and Violence* (1979). A sweeping reappraisal of the church's teaching on violence.

Steiner, Susan Clemmer. *Joining the Army That Sheds No Blood* (1982). The case for biblical pacifism written for teens.

Wenger, J. C. *The Way of Peace* (1977). A brief treatment of Christ's teachings and the way of peace through the centuries.

Yoder, John H. *What Would You Do?* (1983). A serious answer to a standard question.

FOR CHILDREN

Bauman, Elizabeth Hershberger, *Coals of Fire* (1954). Stories of people who returned good for evil.

Moore, Ruth Nulton. *Peace Treaty* (1977). A historical novel involving the efforts of Moravian missionary Christian Frederick Post to bring peace to the Ohio Valley in 1758.

Smucker, Barbara Claassen. *Henry's Red Sea* (1955). The dramatic escape of 1,000 Russian Mennonites from Berlin following World War II.